DOES THE ARMY HAVE A NATIONAL LAND USE STRATEGY?

David Rubenson

Robert Weissler

Carolyn Wong

Robert Everson

Prepared for the United States Army

Arroyo Center

RAND

Approved for public release; distribution unlimited

For more information on the RAND Arroyo Center, contact the Director of Operations, (310) 393-0411, extension 6500, or visit the Arroyo Center's Web site at http://www.rand.org/organization/ard/

PREFACE

This report documents the findings of a project related to Army land policy and approaches to fulfilling Army needs for training lands. The Army has been criticized for its lack of a comprehensive land-use strategy to guide decisions and help set priorities for land policy initiatives. This document reviews the Army's current approach to establishing requirements and evaluates the policy changes that might occur with a comprehensive strategy. It differs from previous assessments in that it explicitly considers the political environment for Army land use.

This report should be of interest to those concerned with Army environmental policy and questions of land use and military training. It should also be of interest to those concerned with potential future Base Realignments and Closures (BRACs) and the forthcoming efforts to renew three large Army parcels under Public Law 99-606. Large land parcels at Fort Bliss and two Alaska bases will be returned to the public domain unless Congress renews 99-606 by the year 2001.

The work was sponsored by Dr. Andrew Vliet, Director of Plans and Programs at Fort Bliss. The research was conducted in the Force Development and Technology Program of RAND Arroyo Center, a federally funded research and development center sponsored by the United States Army.

CONTENTS

SUMMARY

The United States military has a long-term need to access land for training, testing, and other military functions. As a result, numerous military installations are involved in land initiatives aimed at preserving or expanding military land holdings. However, critics claim that declining defense budgets should reduce the need for military land. They argue that there is an aggregate oversupply of military land and that there has been a failure to optimize use. Military land initiatives are seen as driven by an inability to share resources among different military organizations. The critics see the military as indulging in "land grabs" instead of relying on a comprehensive land-use strategy that sets priorities for land initiatives. In this view, the military seems unable to determine its aggregate land needs.

The purpose of this report is to explore this criticism of military land-use policy and determine how the Department of Defense can most appropriately respond. We focus on Army needs and processes, but the implications are relevant to all the services. The issue is critical because 30 percent of DoD lands will come under congressional scrutiny in 2001 with the expiration of the 1986 Military Lands Withdrawal Act. This could coincide with an additional round of the Base Realignment and Closure (BRAC) process. Together, these two activities could constitute a review of the entire military basing structure.

We begin by analyzing the organizational and physical boundaries within the DoD and Army land base. We show how the DoD land base is divided among the military services (Army, Navy, Air Force, and Marine Corps) and by numerous organizational boundaries within each service. The Army's land is divided among several major commands, subcommands, and installations. At each level, intra-agency organizational boundaries separate the land manager and land user.

At the installation level, the organizational boundaries typically coincide with the physical boundaries, since most installations are physically isolated. We show that most Army soldiers and infrastructure are located on small installations in the East. These are far from the large empty ranges in the West, which constitute the bulk of Army lands. The latter have been used for testing new weapon systems and are now underutilized.

We then review the Army's methodology for determining land needs. This methodology compares an installation's needs with the land it has available; it does not consider aggregate Army lands. The methodology tends to exaggerate needs because it does not consider the implicit strategy that the land users employ to cope with land shortfalls. The discrepancy is a product of the intraorganizational lines between land users and land managers. Nevertheless, almost all active units are based on small installations that would benefit from additional land, even if that land is not as critical as the Army's formal methodology implies it has to be.

One technique used to overcome land deficiencies on small Eastern installations is to visit the National Training Center (NTC) in the Mojave Desert. This suggests that the other large, underutilized Western ranges could be used to offset additional land shortages. However, we show that the costs of moving units for such temporary training are prohibitive and much more onerous than any of the organizational obstacles to using these ranges. Units will pay to visit NTC because of the numerous other training benefits, in addition to the large land areas, that NTC provides.

We then consider the possibility of setting priorities for Army land initiatives. We discuss three of the most important land initiatives of the last fifteen years and show that the military significance of each initiative had little to do with the ultimate outcome. Instead, the availability of the land and local political support were the primary elements of success or failure. Given that additional land will benefit a significant subset of Army installations (virtually all those housing active units), it is rational for the Army to use feasibility of acquisition as the primary factor for determining whether to pursue a land initiative.

We then discuss the role of simulation technology and BRAC in meeting future land needs. Both BRAC and simulation offer the possibility of overcoming the physical boundaries that divide the DoD land base. However, the Army tends not to evaluate either process for its implications on land use. The organizational boundaries between those monitoring land issues and those responsible for BRAC and simulation must be overcome to develop an effective long-term land-use strategy.

We conclude that the Army has a coherent land-use strategy today, but it is an implicit one, and it has not been explained inside or outside the Army. Physical boundaries prevent a true optimization of Army land use and make the subject of "total Army land needs" into a meaningless concept. We also conclude that there is a broad subset of Army installations that would benefit from additional land and that a policy of protecting and acquiring lands for those installations when feasible is a rational one. Among this subset, the constraints imposed by land-use politics make efforts to set priorities essentially meaningless.

We also emphasize that the implicit strategy is only relevant given the political constraints on base closure and realignment. The Army does not have a strategy for determining its long-range basing needs should it be allowed to make fundamental changes in its basing structure.

We recommend that the Army and the military publish a national land strategy in an effort to explain the constraints described above. Such a strategy would not change decisionmaking, but it would help clarify the need for land despite the drop in the overall defense budget. To do this, the Army would need to overcome the organizational boundaries that exist between land managers and land users and begin to evaluate the land-use implications of simulation technology and BRAC.

In summary, we find that current Army land use policies are driven by physical boundaries. However, the Army's ability to explain those policies and to plan for future developments are affected by organizational boundaries.

Chapter One

INTRODUCTION

Figure 1

Figure 1 illustrates the title of this report, which is presented as an annotated briefing. The Army and the Department of Defense (DoD) have been criticized for the lack of a systematic approach to determining training land requirements and for the failure to set priorities among training land initiatives. The purpose of this report is to review the Army's current approach to assessing land requirements and to determine the validity and impact of the critiques.

A central issue is whether current policies lead to efficient land use or whether internal Army organizational boundaries divide land resources in inefficient ways and create a need for additional land. In other words, does the division of Army lands among major internal organizational entities (commands, subcommands, and installations) create obstacles to efficient sharing of land resources? Although our focus is on the Army, we will also ask similar questions about the Army's ability to access Air Force and Navy lands. This is important because much of the public views military land as a single resource.

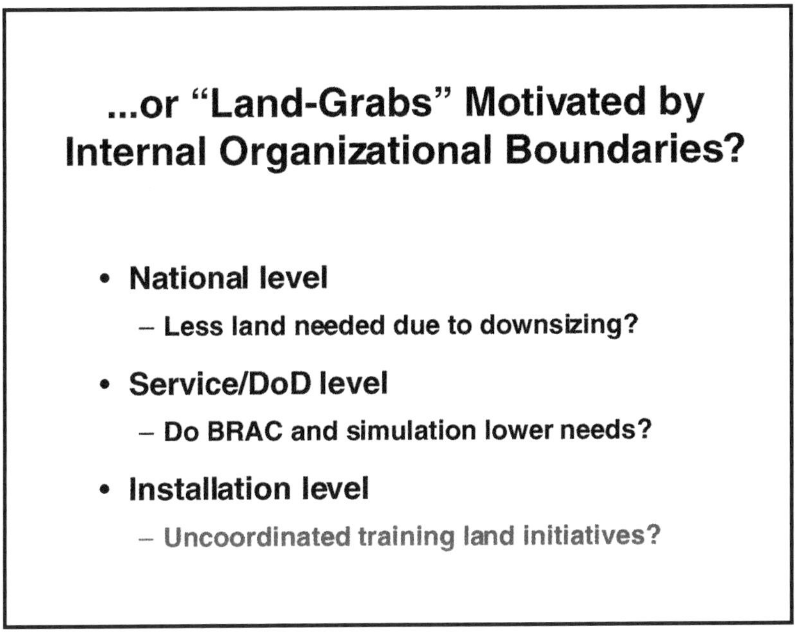

Figure 2

The title of Figure 2 continues the sentence in Figure 1 by presenting a critic's view of Army (DoD) land use policy. It suggests that Army land use strategy is a product of the inability of one part of the organization to understand the needs and actions of others. Figure 2 also suggests part of the outline of this briefing. In the first half of the report, we develop a "strawman" criticism of the Army's land use strategy. Previous studies by government agencies and comments by advocacy groups are the basis for this critique. We then analyze the validity of the critique.

At a broad level of national policy, the end of the Cold War and declining DoD budgets have created the perception that there is less need for military land.[1] This perception has been enhanced by re-

[1]Although our focus is on Army policy, the public's perception of Army land policy is linked to its perception of the entire military, hence we refer to the DoD budget rather than the Army budget. More generally, the critique of Army land policy has also been

peated pleas from the Secretary of Defense for additional rounds of Base Realignment and Closure (BRAC). Many assume that the desire to close bases (and the corresponding land holdings) indicates that the DoD has more than enough land.

The DoD and the military services have also been aggressively funding training-simulation initiatives. These technologies offer the possibility of reducing land needs by allowing training in a simulated environment. This feeds the critics' arguments, and moreover we found that a not insignificant number of DoD and Army policymakers believe such simulations will significantly reduce future land use needs.

Despite these developments, several Army (and Navy and Air Force) installations are pursuing land initiatives aimed at preserving or expanding their land holdings. These initiatives are primarily for training land, as opposed to land for testing new weapon systems. Testing and training are the dominant uses of military lands, though there are smaller land uses for logistics, the reserve components, offices, and other military functions.

The seeming inconsistency between installation-level actions and perceptions of national-level trends suggests to some that the Army does not have a coordinated land strategy. It suggests that even if individual installations have land deficiencies, the Army, or the military more generally, have adequate resources that can and should be used to offset local needs.

It also suggests that internal organizational boundaries define the Army (and the DoD) approach. By this we mean that each installation assesses its needs without considering Army-wide (or DoD-wide) needs and resources. Bureaucratic obstacles are seen to make it difficult to share land among Army organizations or between Army organizations and those of the Air Force and Navy. The critique also suggests that headquarters has failed to properly integrate national needs and resources. At worst, all these perceptions confirm the no-

---

applied to that of the other services and the military as a single entity. So though our focus is on Army land policy, we examine this policy in the context of the entire military land resource and suggest that the Air Force and the Navy face similar issues.

tion that the military merely seeks to acquire land whenever it can and is involved in a series of "land grabs."[2]

Given the perceived contradiction outlined in Figure 2, this briefing will attempt to answer the following policy questions:

- Why is it important to have a coherent national military land strategy?
- What organizational boundaries divide DoD land resources? What physical boundaries?
- How does the Army determine land needs, and how would a strategy that minimizes the role of organizational boundaries change decisionmaking?
- How much land does the Army need?
- How will these answers change with new developments in simulation technology or with additional rounds of BRAC?

The approach used in this report is to develop answers to these questions in the context of the Army's need for training lands for the active Army. Although testing requires vast spaces of land, overall test activity has dropped since the end of the Cold War. We will consider the needs of the active Army in the context of the entire training and test land resource. The reserve component is also a user of lands but will do much of its large-scale training on installations used by the active Army. If installations are sized properly for the active Army, they should be adequate for the reserves. Depots, offices, arsenals, and other Army functions occupy land but generally require only small parcels.

---

[2]The term "land grab" or "military land grab" has been used by a variety of critics. See, for example, Coman McCarthy, "The Pentagon's Land Sighting," *Washington Post*, January 21, 1990. The term was also used in conjunction with the Army's interest in a land exchange at Camp Shelby, Mississippi; see *Biloxi Sun Herald*, January 22, 1990.

Chapter Two

IMPORTANCE OF A NATIONAL STRATEGY

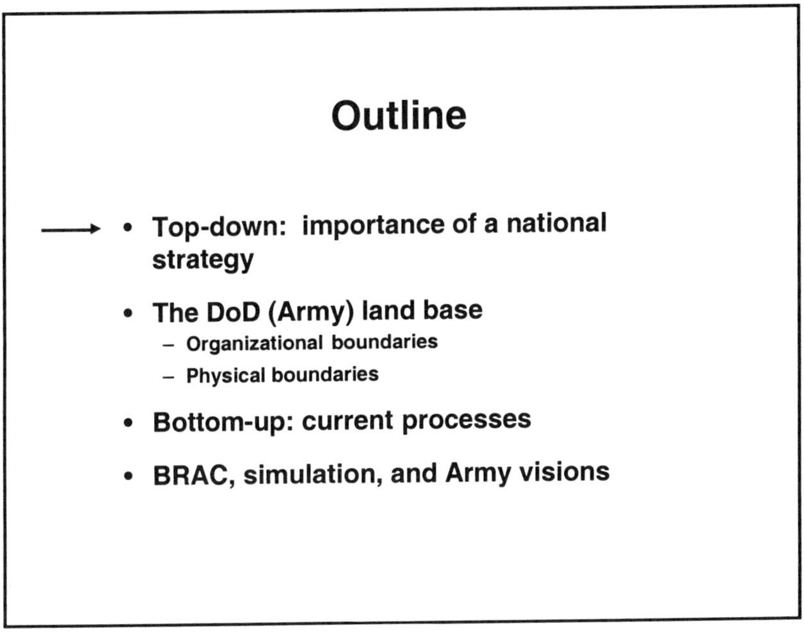

Figure 3

Figure 3 presents an outline of the briefing that corresponds to the policy questions discussed below Figure 2. In this section we describe the military and political importance of a coherent national military land strategy and amplify on why critics cite internal DoD organizational boundaries as an obstacle to coherence.

Next we shall describe the Army and DoD land resource and the physical and organizational boundaries that divide it. We include the DoD land resource because we consider obstacles to Army use of these lands.

In a subsequent section we shall move from a focus on the overall military land resource to the Army's process for determining land requirements and responding to perceived land shortages. We analyze how decisionmaking would be affected by an approach that overcomes internal organizational boundaries.

Finally, we shall describe how simulation technology and BRAC might change the role of such a strategy.

Intense Competition for Land

- A post-1950 problem
  - Large Cold War "withdrawals"
  - 1959 Engle Act
- Less land
  - Suburban sprawl
  - Proliferation of user groups in West
- User groups well organized
  - Locally
  - Washington
- Environmental law invites public review

Figure 4

Figure 4 and the following discussion provide an abbreviated summary of the policy issues related to military use of public lands. The broad implication is that any military request for land will be carefully scrutinized and may be opposed by groups with alternative claims for use of the land.

EASY MILITARY ACCESS TO PUBLIC LANDS (1800–1950)

The United States military manages approximately 24 million acres of federal land, and the U.S. Army manages about half of this total. Throughout much of our history there has been little public concern about how much land the military needed or how the military managed land. The origins of many Army bases date back to the Indian wars, the Civil War, and beyond. These older bases are small, and many are located in the eastern half of the country. In the era between the world wars, motorized combat vehicles, aircraft, and long-range artillery were introduced into the military. The Cold War brought still faster and longer-range weapon systems such as missiles, jet aircraft, helicopters, and faster armored vehicles. Vast spaces were needed to develop and test these new weapons. To meet this need, the executive branch tapped into the vast federal land assets in the West and the Southwest by "withdrawing" the needed lands from the public domain. Withdrawal means removing lands from the public domain and transferring management to the military. The size and low population of the West, along with the urgency of the military missions, minimized public concerns.

GROWING CONSTRAINTS (1950–TODAY)

One of the first indications of changing societal attitudes occurred in 1957, when a New Mexico rancher offered armed resistance to Army efforts to confiscate land on what is now the McGregor Range within Fort Bliss. The episode at the Praether ranch was later immortalized in Edward Abbey's novel *Fire on the Mountain.* The incident highlighted the growing concerns about the executive branch's ability to unilaterally seize land for military purposes. These concerns culminated in the 1959 Engle Act, which requires congressional approval for withdrawals of more than 5,000 acres of public land for military purposes.

The Engle Act was only the beginning of closer monitoring of military land needs and management. The numerous environmental laws of the early 1970s, such as the National Environmental Policy Act (NEPA), the Endangered Species Act, the Clean Water Act, and the Clean Air Act, indicated society's desire to monitor the environmental consequences of all private and public activity. Although there was initially little enforcement on military bases, this situation began to change in the mid-1980s. By the mid-1990s the military was paying about $5.0 billion annually to ensure compliance with environmental statues.[3] The imposition of restrictions on military training at

---

[3]Army environmental spending was only $570 million in fiscal year (FY) 1990, reached $1.744 billion by FY95, and declined to $1.575 billion in FY97. See *The Army Budget,* an annual publication by the Army Budget Office. In FY99 the Army is projected to spend about $1.2 billion for environmental programs. The recent trend toward declining costs is driven by the substantial capital expenditures made earlier to solve long-

Fort Bragg due to the Endangered Species Act demonstrated that these laws could override concerns about readiness and training effectiveness.[4] Endangered species concerns have been greatest on the small Eastern bases where suburban sprawl has reached the edges of bases and where there are few other federal lands for habitat.

An equally important trend has been the rapid demographic growth in the Western states where the federal government's Bureau of Land Management manages extensive tracts. The military's ability to access these lands was dramatically reduced in the 1980s when rapid population growth hit the region. Most of this growth occurred in cities and not on the vast tracts of public lands. This has left the politics of land use in a deceptively complex situation. Although most of the West still appears to be empty, new categories of urban recreational users such as hikers, river rafters, fly fishermen, off-road vehicle users, preservationists, and others now compete with the traditional ranching and forestry interests for use of the public domain. These groups, old and new, are well organized and well represented in state capitals and Washington, D.C.

This demographic change has had important implications for the military. Requests for land are now scrutinized in detail and often opposed by well-organized groups. These constituencies review military documents justifying the need for land and have demonstrated the ability to fight proposals in both Congress and the courts. One of the most effective tools is the National Environmental Policy Act (NEPA), which requires analysis of environmental impacts, Environmental Impact Statements (EISs), and public hearings for any major federal decision. Although NEPA does not mandate the outcome of a decisionmaking process, its complex protocols do allow opponents of federal decisions to access the courts and force federal agencies to redo all or part of the NEPA process. The required public meetings can be a rallying event for diverse groups opposed to a particular decision.

---

festering environmental problems. The reduced costs are also the product of less activity associated with lower overall Army budgets.

[4]See David Rubenson, Jerome Aroesty, and Charles Thompsen, *Two Shades of Green: Environmental Protection and Combat Training*, Santa Monica, CA: RAND, R-4220-A, 1992, for a description of the process that occurred at Fort Bragg.

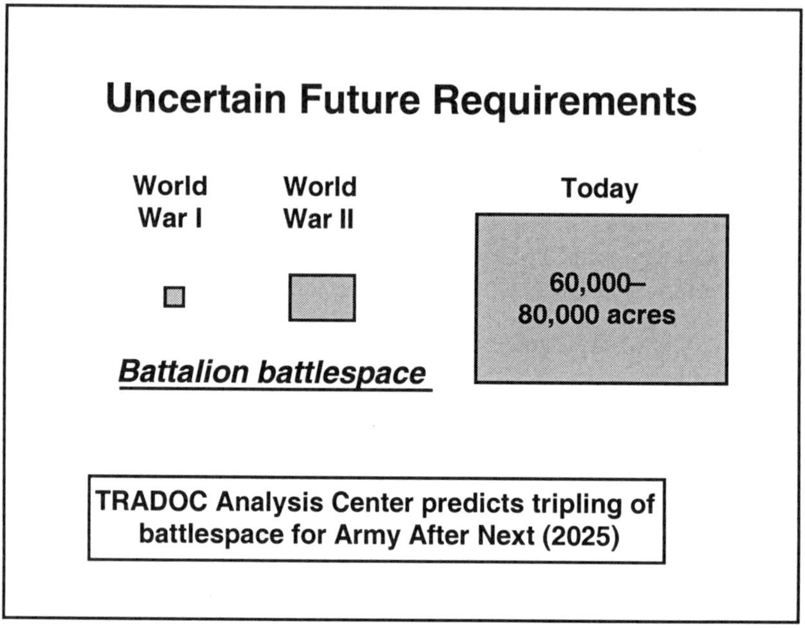

Figure 5

Figure 5 indicates that despite the growing competition for land, the Army and the DoD face a long-term challenge of ensuring that there is enough land for training and testing. The primary factor creating this challenge is the continuing increase in the span and tempo of warfare. Figure 5 shows the relative battlespace for forces of three different eras. A World War II battalion could be expected to fight in an area of about 4,000 acres.[5] During World War I there was significantly less mobility and an even smaller battlespace. Today, longer-range weapon systems, longer-range target acquisition systems, and increased mobility have increased the size of the expected battlespace. Army Training Circular 25-1 (last updated in 1991) now states that an armored battalion requires 60,000 acres to train.

---

[5]Anne Chapman, *The National Training Center Matures 1985–1993*, TRADOC Historical Monograph Series, Military History Office, U.S. Army Training and Doctrine Command, 1997, p. 87.

Environmental restrictions imply that even more land would be required to meet that demand in a peacetime training mode. Many installations have set aside areas to satisfy laws such as the Endangered Species Act and other statutes involving the conservation of natural resources. As a result, the Army's total land requirements will often exceed the amount of land it actually uses.

ARMY XXI

Army XXI represents ongoing efforts to modernize the Army's existing force.[6] While the vision includes factors beyond those determining battlespace, such as leadership training, distance learning, and restatements of Army values and roles, its implications for battlespace promise a continuation of the historical trend. The Army hopes that it can fully implement the vision by 2010.

The main impact on the parameters described above will come from the goal of supplementing existing weapon systems with new capabilities derived from information technology. The Army hopes to develop a form of *information dominance* that will eliminate some of the "fog and friction" of war and enable the Army's forces to take a quantum leap relative to today's capability.

Military planners currently anticipate that information dominance will facilitate a concept called *Dominant Maneuver.* As defined in the Army's *Vision 2010* document,

> Dominant Maneuver will be the multidimensional application of information, engagement, and mobility capabilities to position and employ widely dispersed joint air, land, sea, and space forces to accomplish assigned operational tasks.

The Army envisions itself moving faster, assembling units quickly from wide areas, and disassembling them with equal speed. It sees itself being able to gain pictures of the battlespace at greater depths and take action at those depths. All of these factors imply a dramatic increase in the battlespace and potentially greater impacts on the land used for training the Army XXI force.

---

[6]See *Army Vision 2010,* Department of the Army.

ARMY AFTER NEXT

Army After Next is an ongoing planning process that is examining concepts and ideas for Army forces beyond those being modified for the Army XXI concept. Army planners hope that the ideas can be implemented in the 2025 time period. Although concepts are still being debated, most Army After Next planning points to the use of lighter and significantly faster forces:

> To achieve the speed of maneuver to wage 21st century knowledge-based warfare will require a new concept of mechanized warfare that will free forces of maneuver inhibiting restrictions. The exploitation of knowledge via increased air and ground mobility will result in unprecedented tactical and operational maneuverability. [7]

The dependence on maneuver has so far led Army planners to consider significantly lighter vehicles, such as a 15-ton, two-man tank, that can gain increased speeds. Heavy lift helicopters and tilt-rotors that could move these light armored vehicles across a fluid and continually reforming battlefield are also being considered.

It is too early to predict how Army After Next will affect training land requirements. However, the current ideas point to the need for vastly larger areas, though possibly with lighter units having less impact on the land. It is also possible that the large areas might not have to be contiguous. Many Army After Next concepts point to rapid insertion of light forces followed by equally rapid removal. A series of military land islands might support Army After Next training just as well as large contiguous blocks of land.

While both Army After Next and Army XXI may yet go through substantial modifications, both concepts point to vastly increased battlespace. As indicated in Figure 5, the TRADOC Analysis Center at one point predicted that certain Army After Next concepts might lead to a tripling of the battlespace by 2025.

---

[7]MG Robert Scales, Jr., and Dr. J. Parmentola, "The Army After Next," *Army RD&A*, May–June 1998.

ALTERNATIVES

Given the uncertainties in the future force structure of the Army, it would be careless not to point out that some ideas may lead to smaller battlespace. Some strategists see the future Army as moving away from large maneuver warfare toward a force trained for more compact battles in urban environments. Some see an emphasis on peacekeeping operations. However, under the assumptions that large maneuver warfare remains an Army priority and that the Army will continue to need to conduct realistic multiechelon field training, trends in technology and tactics point to the need for larger expanses of training land.

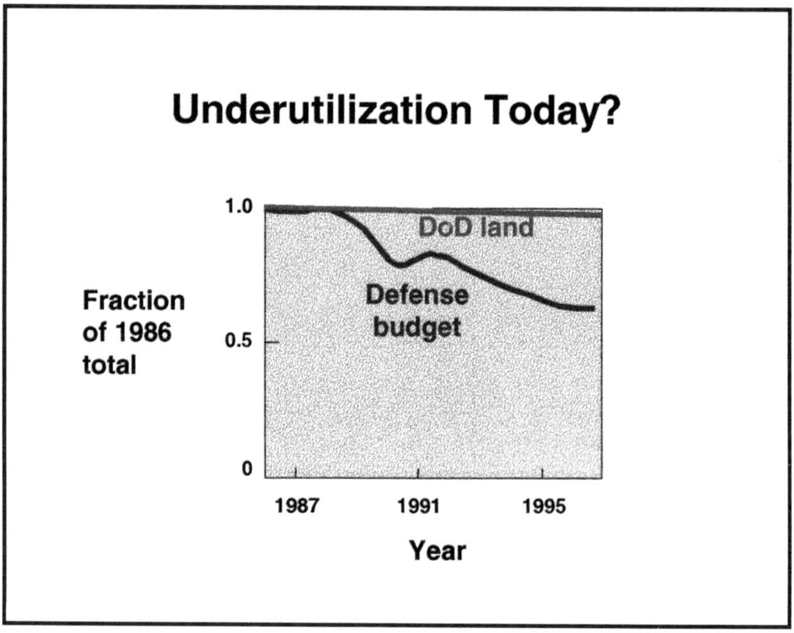

Figure 6

While Figure 5 suggests the eventual need for more land, Figure 6 suggests a possible overabundance today. Despite steep declines in the defense budget (measured in constant dollars), the DoD manages roughly the same amount of land it did 15 years ago. Although numerous bases have been closed, only a tiny fraction of the DoD Cold War land base has been returned to the public domain.[8] The chart suggests that military lands are, in aggregate, underutilized. With the budget and number of soldiers shrinking, there are fewer units with fewer dollars for training and testing.

---

[8]An interesting question is whether the utilization of lands used for training the active Army (as opposed to weapons testing, training the reserves, or other noncombat training activity) has decreased as well. In FY86 there were 11 active divisions stationed within the lower 48 states, 1 each in Alaska and Hawaii, and 5 abroad. By FY96 there was the equivalent of approximately 9 divisions in the lower 48 and 1 abroad. Thus the number of units based in the lower 48 states has not dropped as dramatically as that in the overall Army.

We used the DoD budget and land resource in Figure 6 (as opposed to Army values for these parameters) because the public perceives the issue as a question of *military* land use. The internal organizational boundaries within the DoD are largely irrelevant to people concerned with public lands. In addition, we are interested in understanding the impact of Army land needs if the bureaucratic obstacles to using any part of the entire DoD land resource could be removed.

As will be discussed in the next figure, the Army is engaged in several land initiatives to preserve or expand the current land base. The need might be explained in two ways. The Army might be maximizing its land holdings in preparation for an uncertain future requirement, but with little basis in today's needs. This would be viewed by some as prudent hedging and by others as a tie-up of unneeded lands. A different explanation may lie with boundaries that divide both the DoD's 24-million-acre land base and the organization that manages it. Individual organizations within DoD may be land deficient while others are in surplus. Whereas some inside DoD may see this as justification for additional land, those concerned with public land use tend to view the military as a single user of a single resource.

Local Army Training Land Initiatives: "Land Grabs" or True Needs?

- Recent expansions
  - Fort Bragg (10,000 acres)
  - Yakima (53,000)
- Proposed expansions
  - Orchard (40,000)
  - Irwin (160,000–332,000)
  - Kentucky (10,000)
- Reclassifications
  - Fort Polk (45,000)
  - Hawaii (8,000)
- Renewals (2001)
  - Bliss (608,000)
  - Alaska (871,000)

Figure 7

As discussed in Figure 2, installations are involved in numerous land initiatives aimed at preserving or expanding the Army's base of training lands. Figure 7 summarizes recent and ongoing Army land initiatives.

The figure shows that not all initiatives involve expansion. Land reclassifications involve change in ownership status or change in use patterns on lands that are leased or borrowed. Withdrawn lands are lands that have been removed from the public domain but could be returned depending on the length of the withdrawal.

The land initiatives of the other military services are not included in Figure 7. These are critical for the Army because the public and regional political leaders may not discriminate among military organizations when judging the fairness and honesty of the land initiative process. The just-completed Air Force efforts to acquire land near Mountain Home Air Force Base in Idaho galvanized opposition groups in many Western states. Another important initiative is the Navy's goal of withdrawing an additional 127,000 acres of public land at Fallon Naval Air Station (NAS) in northern Nevada. The proposal has drawn opposition from the state of Nevada and from local groups. The controversy is important for the Army because the Bravo 20 bombing range at Fallon is one of the six ranges that Congress will need to renew by 2001.

Below we give a brief description of each of the major Army land initiatives. Some will be discussed in greater detail later in the text. There are numerous smaller initiatives involving a few hundred acres or less. These are generally motivated by the need to rationalize local boundaries rather than by efforts to reconfigure installations to perform new or expanded missions.

Fort Bragg

Fort Bragg is home to the XVIII Airborne Corps headquarters and the 82nd Airborne Division, which operates on an 18-hour deployment notice and is typically among the first units to be involved in an Army contingency. The 82nd is a light unit with few tracked vehicles. Fort Bragg is also home to the North Carolina National Guard with its heavier military mission involving M-1 tanks.

Fort Bragg has had what is certainly the nation's most serious conflict between environmental priorities and the need for military training. Efforts to preserve the red-cockaded woodpecker (RCW), a listed species under the federal Endangered Species Act, have resulted in significant restrictions on military operations. As part of an effort to reduce restrictions, Fort Bragg recently acquired 10,546 acres of private land adjacent to the installation at a cost of approximately $30 million. The acquisition expands Bragg's RCW habitat, allowing additional environmental management options and possibly leading to greater flexibility for training on the remainder of the installation. However, the NEPA process for the acquisition did not include military activities, and additional analysis and documentation would be required to enable them.

Yakima

In conjunction with the development of the Yakima Firing Range as a regional training center for units at Fort Lewis, the Army acquired an additional 55,000 acres of maneuver training land in the early 1990s.

Orchard

The Orchard Training Area comprises 125,000 acres of land that is used by the Idaho National Guard. Use of the land is ensured by a series of agreements between the Guard and the federal Bureau of Land Management and state land management agencies.

The entire Orchard Training Center is located in an area classified as a National Conservation Area. Orchard's efforts to monitor long-run environmental trends have led to the conclusion that ecological health would be improved by spreading training effects over a larger area. Orchard has therefore begun the process of acquiring up to an additional 40,000 acres by extending agreements with the relevant government agencies. The initiative is in the early stages and is currently awaiting Department of the Army approval before proceeding.

JRTC/Polk[9]

Fort Polk is the home of the 2nd Armored Cavalry Regiment (ACR) and the Joint Readiness Training Center (JRTC). The Army role of the JRTC will be discussed in Figure 24.

The main post at Fort Polk consists of three contiguous blocks of land. The northern parcel contains 67,000 acres of Army land. Directly to the south is 40,000 acres of U.S. Forest Service Land that the Army has agreements to use and where Army activities take priority over traditional Forest Service multiple-use activities. Still further to the south is another 45,000 acres of Forest Service land where the Army has rights to conduct limited activities and where traditional

---

[9]Most of this discussion is based on information in the *DRAFT Environmental Assessment for Increased Military Training Use of the Vernon Ranger District, Kisatchie National Forest,* Fort Polk, Louisiana, February 1998.

Forest Service multiple-use activities take priority. This is referred to as a Low Use Area (LUA).

The current proposal is to modify the existing agreement in the LUA to increase the frequency of activities and to introduce six new activities that are currently prohibited. The reason for the initiative is that currently available land is not sufficient to meet doctrinal requirements. The new uses would be cross-country vehicle maneuvers, blackout driving, pyrotechnics, construction of hasty defensive systems, emplacement of obstacles, and establishment of support areas. The proposal would limit multiple-use activities to ensure that minimum Army training needs are fulfilled.

Fort Polk and the Forest Service issued an Environmental Assessment in February 1998.

Irwin/NTC

Fort Irwin is the home of the 11th ACR and the National Training Center (NTC), where force-on-force exercises can occur and be monitored and evaluated with the support of sophisticated instrumentation and expert control and evaluation methods. The NTC does not meet doctrinal requirements for full brigade operations and has been trying to acquire additional land for almost 15 years. Currently, brigade (–) operations, consisting of two battalions and brigade-level support units, are conducted at NTC. The major obstacles to the land expansion have been the need to protect the desert tortoise, which is a listed species under the Endangered Species Act, and the complicated land politics in the Mojave Desert. Additional background will be presented in Figure 33.

Kentucky

The Kentucky National Guard is attempting to purchase 10,000 acres of private land to supplement an 8,000-acre training area in western Kentucky. The Guard hopes to be able to perform battalion-level tank maneuvers. It is interesting to note that 18,000 acres would be approximately a factor of three smaller than required by official Army doctrine (TC 25-1) for conducting tank battalion maneuvers.

The initiative will be paid for from state funds.

Hawaii

This is an initiative to purchase approximately 8,000 of acres of land that is currently leased by the Army's Schofield Barracks.

McGregor

The McGregor Range constitutes approximately 700,000 of Fort Bliss's 1,200,000 acres. 600,000 acres of McGregor were withdrawn under Public Law 99-606. Fort Bliss has prepared a draft Environmental Impact Statement (EIS) and an application for renewal of the range. Congress must renew the range by 2001 or it will revert to the public domain. The local Bureau of Land Management office favors the return of about 270,000 acres to BLM management. Public meetings have been sparsely attended, and the community has not voiced any significant support for such a return.

McGregor is the Army's primary land area used for training air defense units. It is also used for the joint and international annual Roving Sands exercise, which has the goal of insuring interoperability among different air defense units.

As this document was going to press, the Senate had approved language authorizing a 50-year renewal of McGregor.

Alaskan Ranges

More than 800,000 acres at Forts Wainwright and Greely were also withdrawn under Public Law 99-606, and the Army has prepared a draft EIS and a renewal application for congressional consideration. Army officials reported "no public or agency concerns expressed during scoping which could be detrimental to withdrawal renewal." The Alaska ranges are the primary training area for the 172nd Infantry Brigade and are the national centers for Arctic training.

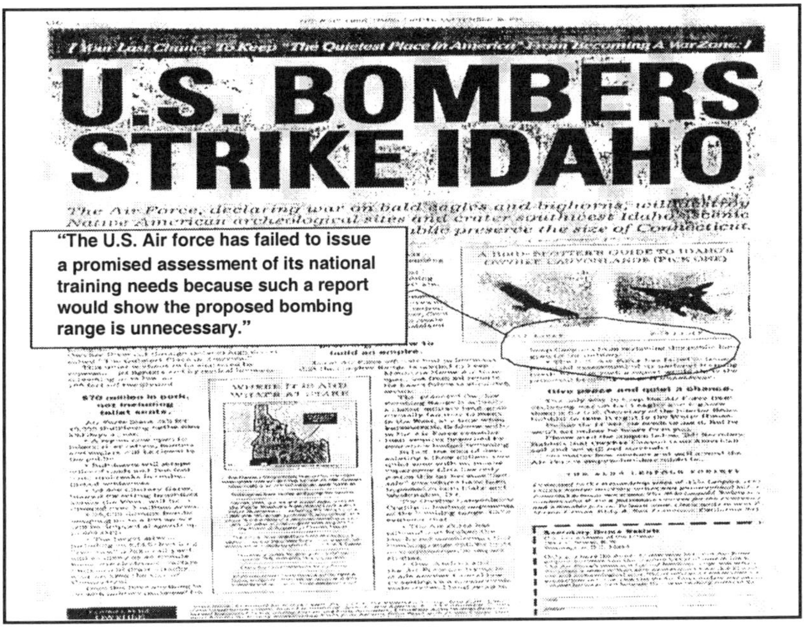

Figure 8

Figure 8 provides a graphic illustration of the political controversy that military land issues can arouse. It reemphasizes the political significance of having a comprehensive national strategy. The figure is a reproduction of a full-page advertisement from the September 30, 1994, Western Edition of the *New York Times*. The ad was sponsored by a consortium of groups trying to block U.S. Air Force plans to build a 25,000-acre bombing range on public lands near Mountain Home Air Force Base in Idaho. The consortium consisted of an unusual mix of ranchers, environmentalists, Native Americans, and others bound by a common desire to block Air Force plans for the new range. We describe this initiative in greater detail in Figure 33.

While the banner headline highlights the emotional reaction, the highlighted text suggests a more thoughtful analytical critique. It suggests that had the Air Force developed a national needs assessment, the new bombing range would not have been necessary. The critics argued that national Air Force resources could offset local needs.

The critique displayed in Figure 8 has been applied to the Army as well and reaffirmed in studies by several government agencies.[10] These studies offered the following criticisms of Army land policy:

1. The Army does not consider "Army-wide" land when considering the needs at individual installations.
2. Land shortages are rarely cited as a factor inhibiting readiness.
3. Current land initiatives (Figure 7) appear to be driven by "targets of opportunity"[11] rather than a rational set of "Army-wide" priorities.

Each has an implication similar to the critique offered in the caption highlighted in Figure 8: the Army needs to analyze land requirements at a national level. The first and third comments point to assessment in the context of all Army land resources, while the second comment calls for embedding land strategy within an overall Army training strategy.

We again emphasize that these arguments represent a critique of current Army and military land policies. We will analyze the validity of this critique in the second half of this report.

---

[10]Army Audit Agency, *Real Estate Acquisitions, Audit Report: AA 98-92*, March 9, 1998. The General Accounting Office issued a series of three studies on Army land requirements: *Army Training: Need to Improve the Assessments of Land Requirements and Priorities*, GAO/NSIAD-90-44BR, December 1989; *Army Training: Computer Simulations Can Improve Command Training in Large-Scale Exercises*, GAO/NSIAD-91-67, January 1991; and *Army Training: Various Factors Create Uncertainty About Need for More Land*, GAO/NSIAD-91-103, April 1991. An additional critical study was issued by the Army Environmental Policy Institute, *Land for Combat Training: A Briefing Book*, June 1996.

[11]"Target of opportunity" was used by the GAO and the Army Audit Agency. It refers to seeking land when it can be acquired as opposed to when it is needed. Its meaning is therefore similar to our use of the term "land grab."

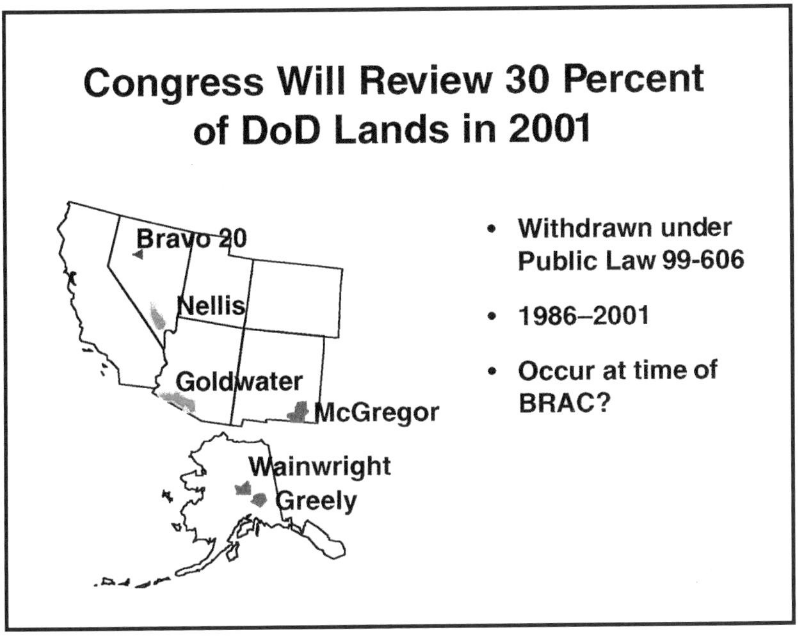

Figure 9

Figure 9 provides an additional reason why the Department of Defense should have a coherent explanation of its national land use strategy. The status of approximately 30 percent of the DoD land base will be reviewed by Congress in conjunction with the expiration of the land withdrawals specified in Public Law 99-606. About 15 percent of the Army's 12 million acres are included in 99-606. This law withdrew six major parcels from the public domain in 1986 for a period of 15 years: Fort Greely, Fort Wainwright, the Nellis Range, the Goldwater Range (Arizona), the Bravo 20 Range at Fallon Naval Air Station (Nevada), and the McGregor Range. At the time this document was going to press, the Senate had passed a 50-year renewal for McGregor. They are all relatively isolated in regions with low population density.

The renewal of these lands is an important legislative priority for the Department of Defense.[12] The three military services have initiated the processes to develop Draft Legislative Environmental Impact Statements (DLEIS) required by the 1986 legislation as a prerequisite for renewal.

Figure 9 also suggests that congressional action related to 99-606 renewals could coincide with another BRAC round. Congress has refused several requests from the Secretary of Defense for additional rounds of BRAC, but there is a general feeling that another BRAC will occur in the not-too-distant future.

The combination of BRAC, 99-606 renewals, and individual initiatives requiring congressional approval (all withdrawals of land more than 5,000 acres) could imply a broad-based review of the DoD basing structure early in the next century. The DoD will want to be able to explain its strategy for making land decisions and be able to answer charges that its strategy is more than just a series of "land grabs" or acquisitions by "target of opportunity."

---

[12]BLM could refuse to accept the lands if they cannot be decontaminated. Although 99-606 is not explicit, we assume that DoD would then be obligated to continue holding the lands. Congress could of course alter this with new legislation.

Do Internal Organizational Boundaries Produce "Land Grabs"?

- Intense competition for land
- Upcoming congressional reviews
  - P.L. 99-606
  - BRAC
  - Individual initiatives
- Aggregate underutilization, installation land initiatives
- Critics charge failure to optimize across land base

Figure 10

Figure 10 summarizes the preceding "strawman" arguments. The figure title repeats the central question of the briefing.

There is now intense competition for land. Efforts to expand the military land base, or even maintain it, are subject to close scrutiny and judged in political processes where internal DoD organizational boundaries are of only minor importance. DoD is typically viewed as a single user of a single resource, and Army policies may be evaluated in the context of that resource.

Criticism of DoD land strategy could be important as Congress considers issues that, taken together, could comprise a review of DoD's entire basing structure. DoD must reconcile the appearance of aggregate underutilization, as illustrated in Figure 6, with requests for additional land. It will need to respond to criticism that current land policy is a set of scattered initiatives driven by internal organizational boundaries that preclude optimization.

This leads to our central policy question. We seek to determine whether internal DoD organizational boundaries, which have little importance in the political arena of public land, produce a situation where the actions of individual Army installations are inconsistent with overall land needs. Do they lead to efforts to acquire land where there is no military need?

Chapter Three

THE DoD AND ARMY LAND BASE

Outline

- Top-down: importance of a national strategy
- → The DoD (Army) land base
  - Organizational boundaries
  - Physical boundaries
- Bottom-up: current processes
  - Installation needs
  - Using underutilized lands
- BRAC, simulation, and Army visions

Figure 11

In this section we review the DoD and Army land base and describe the organizational and physical boundaries that divide it.

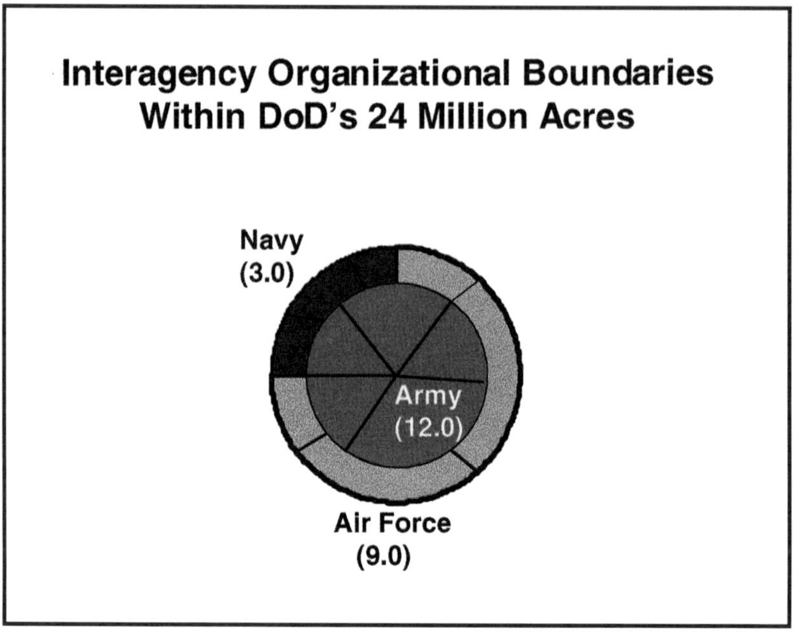

Figure 12

Figure 12 divides the DoD's 24 million acres by major military service. In rough numbers the Army manages 12 million acres, the Navy 3 million (including the Marine Corps), and the Air Force 9 million. The Defense Logistics Agency and other small agencies also manage small parcels of land. We refer to the divisions in Figure 12 as *interagency* organizational boundaries.

The lines within each of the three major categories indicate that each of the military services divides its holdings among major commands.

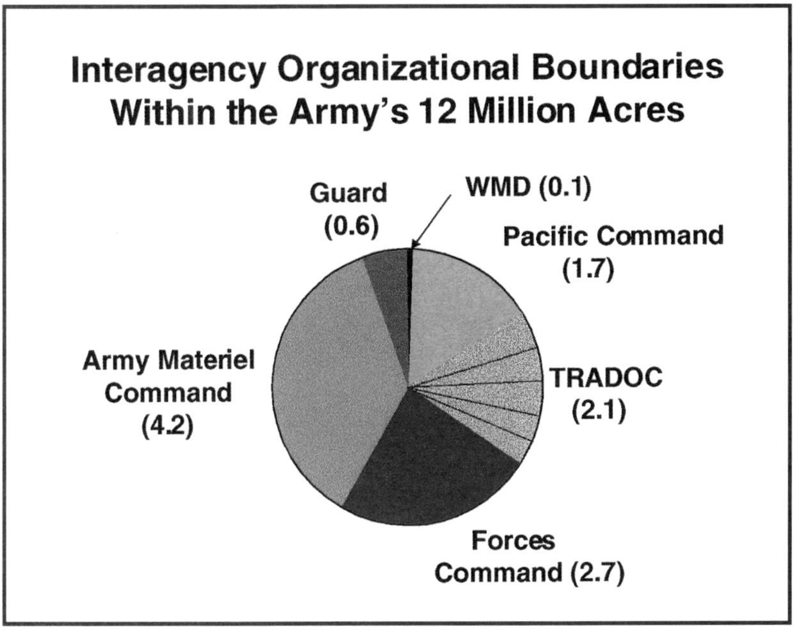

Figure 13

Figure 13 divides the 12-million-acre Army land circle presented in Figure 12 into ownership parcels by major Army command. We again refer to these divisions as "interagency" boundaries.

The Army Materiel Command (AMC) manages more than four million acres and is the Army's largest land manager. AMC contains the Army's industrial base of arsenals, laboratories, and depots. Its major land holdings are several large developmental weapons test ranges. Activity at these ranges has dropped significantly since the end of the Cold War. With the exception of the Jefferson Proving Ground, there have been no closures of major test ranges.

Forces Command houses most of the Army's trained and ready units sustained in CONUS and contains 2.7 million acres. The Training and Doctrine Command (TRADOC) houses the Army schools and comprises 2.1 million acres. The Pacific Command contains bases in Alaska and Hawaii and manages 1.7 million acres. The National

Guard and the Washington Military District contain other numerous small holdings.

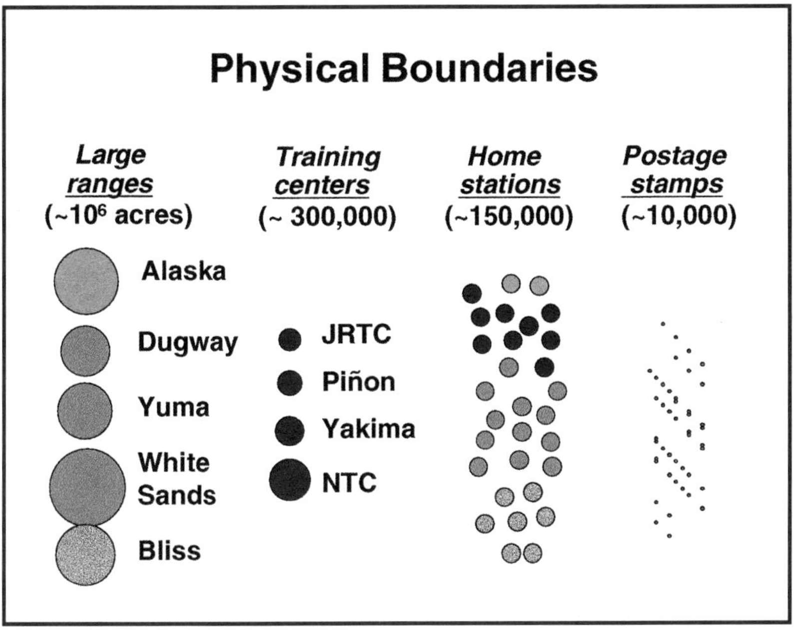

Figure 14

The institutional boundaries shown in Figure 13 can be divided into individual installations. Installations are generally separate organizational and physical entities. White Sands and Fort Bliss (shown connected in Figure 14) are contiguous and therefore represent distinct organizational but not physical entities. The same is true of the Fort Irwin's National Training Center (NTC) and the China Lake Naval Weapons Station, as well as Dugway Proving Ground and the Air Force's Utah Test and Training Range. Figure 14 is limited to Army lands and does not illustrate those last two cases.

Figure 14 displays a schematic of Army installations and divides the installations into four categories. The color code is identical to that of Figure 13, so the division by major command is also illustrated. Circle sizes are to scale. The four categories are "large ranges," "training centers," "home stations," and "postage stamps." The defining concept is size, with the categories representing land areas of approximately 1 million, 300,000, 150,000, and less than 10,000 acres. There is significant variation in each group. The categories are arranged from right to left because, as will be discussed in Figure 16a, they are distributed in a rough east-to-west pattern across the CONUS.

The term "home station" is used because the Forces Command units are housed on bases of roughly 150,000 acres.[13] Other commands also have bases in this size category. Since all the initiatives listed in Figure 7 involve training land, we have chosen the term "home station" for this category because Forces Command units have the most important training land requirements.

The Army has five "large ranges" constituting about half of its total acreage. Three are test ranges belonging to AMC, one is in Alaska, and Fort Bliss is part of TRADOC.

Air Force and Navy installations could also be characterized on a schematic like that of Figure 14. They can be significant for the Army because they may offer the possibility of joint use and because external critics ignore the divisions within the military (organizational boundaries) and assume that such joint use is practical. From this perspective, the most significant Navy and Air Force installations (for the Army) are Edwards Air Force Base, China Lake Naval Weapons Station, the Goldwater Range at Luke Air Force Base, and the Nellis Range. Each of these would be categorized as a "large range" in Figure 14.

---

[13]The largest Forces Command home station is Fort Stewart at 279,000 acres and the smallest is Fort Lewis at 86,000 acres.

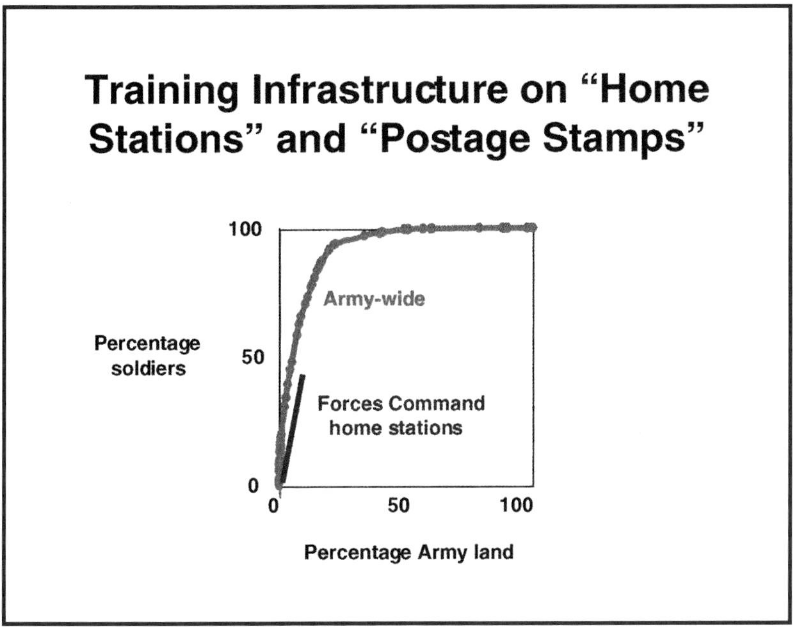

Figure 15

Figure 15 highlights one of the most significant aspects of the physical boundaries described in Figure 14. The Army's soldiers, and hence much of its training infrastructure, are separated from its lands. The chart shows that about 90 percent of the Army's soldiers are assigned to installations comprising only about 15 percent of its lands. This includes lands in CONUS, Alaska, and Hawaii. Most of the Army's infrastructure is located on "home stations" and "postage stamps."

The curve "Army-wide" has been constructed from left to right in the order of density. The most crowded installations represent the nearly vertical left side of the curve. The large empty test ranges comprise the top, or horizontal, part of the curve. Figure 15 also shows how the curve would develop if we had begun with Forces Command home stations only. The close overlap with the steep part of the "Army-wide" curve shows that these home stations include many of the Army's most crowded installations. The Forces Command curve ends at about 10 percent of Army land, corresponding to the fraction of the Army's total contained in these home stations.

Appendix A provides a detailed breakout of the Army's 90 largest installations and is the basis for Figure 15.

Figure 16a

Figure 16a is a map of all military installations in the United States. It highlights the Forces Command home stations. Forces Command training areas, such as Yakima, Piñon Canyon, and the National Training Center, are not highlighted because these posts house few active soldiers. This figure expands the point made in Figure 15 by showing that infrastructure is separated from land by significant distances.

The map shows that most home stations are located far from the large ranges that constitute about half of the Army's and the DoD's land base. The bulk of that land base is in the West and the Southwest, while most of the Army's trained and ready units are based in the East.

There are also Forces Command units housed on TRADOC installations. Most significant are III Corps Artillery stationed at Fort Sill, Oklahoma, the 3rd brigade of the 3rd Infantry Division (mechanized) at Fort Benning, Georgia, and the units at Fort Bliss. The Bliss units constitute all domestically based air defense units at the corps level or above. Fort Bliss is also significant because it is the Army's only "large range" in the lower 48 states that is not part of the AMC. As will be discussed in Figure 28, the organizational boundaries between AMC test ranges and the training portion of the Army have important implications for Army land policy.

Fort Bliss is contiguous with White Sands Missile Range, which is part of AMC, and both comprise the large military land area in southern New Mexico. Figure 16b shows the distance between the Army's active soldiers and Fort Bliss.

Figure 16b shows that there are few troops, other than those stationed at Fort Bliss, within 400 miles of this large land parcel. Forts Sill, Hood, Carson, and Riley are within a 400–500 mile range, and

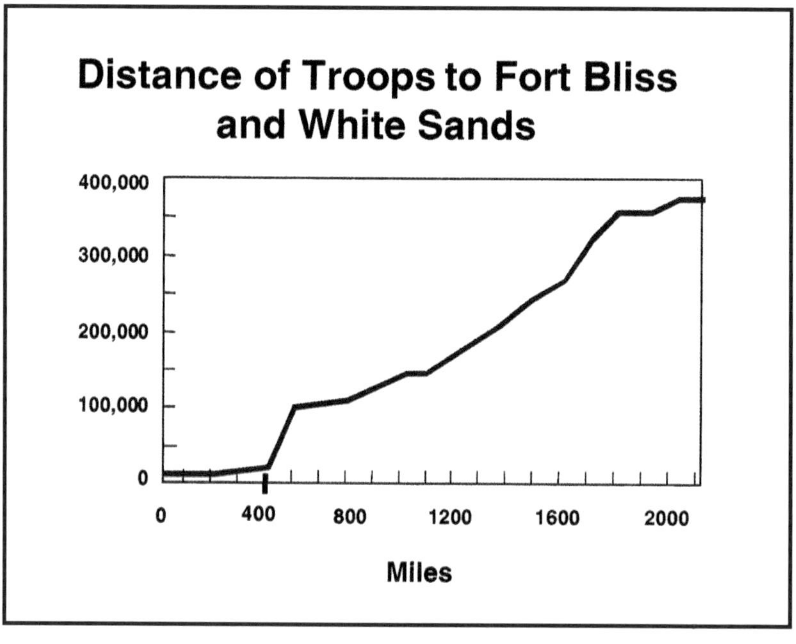

Figure 16b

other units are much farther. The distances between the Army's soldiers and other large ranges would be represented by a similar graph but would be shifted by approximately 500 additional miles.

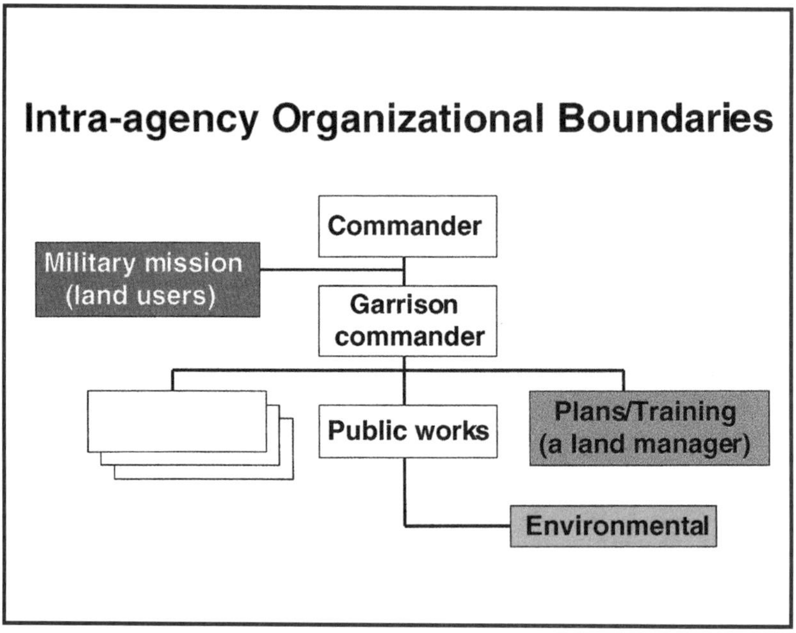

Figure 17

Figure 17 describes the intraorganizational boundaries that can occur within an Army installation. The users of land are the units performing the military mission at an installation. There is no single land manager. The garrison commander is responsible for running the entire installation. Range control schedules the training land and is responsible for some aspects of land maintenance. The environmental office is responsible for negotiating with environmental regulators and developing recommendations and restrictions that ensure compliance with statutes. Public works is responsible for the utilities and buildings in the cantonment and training areas.

The organization displayed in Figure 17 is replicated at the major command, headquarters, and DoD level of the organization. Every office reports through the highest-level on-site military commander at a site. The environmental office at an installation does not report to the environmental office at headquarters. The headquarters environmental office does, however, write policies, rules, and regulations that installation environmental offices are expected to follow. It also plays a role in allocating budgets.

A 1992 RAND report documented the difficulty in crossing the organizational lines shown in Figure 17 to effectively blend training and environmental concerns.[14] Since that time the Army has made great strides in overcoming these boundaries and in ensuring that diverse installation functions are well coordinated. Nevertheless, many procedures, regulations, and policies remain "stovepiped." By this term we mean they are developed by the analogous functional headquarters office and sent to installations down a narrow stovepipe with little regard for related functions. As an example, Army regulation AR 210-21, which governs the process for analyzing an installation's land requirements, is written at headquarters by the Office of the Deputy Chief of Staff for Operations and Plans (ODSCOPS) and implemented at the installation level by the Directorate of Plans and Training. Input from the environmental function only occurs if the installation culture facilitates such interactions. While the Army has made great strides in building a multidisciplinary culture, many of the Army's rules and regulations have changed more slowly.

---

[14]David Rubenson, Jerome Aroesty, and Charles Thompsen, *Two Shades of Green: Environmental Protection and Combat Training*, Santa Monica, CA: RAND, R-4220-A, 1992.

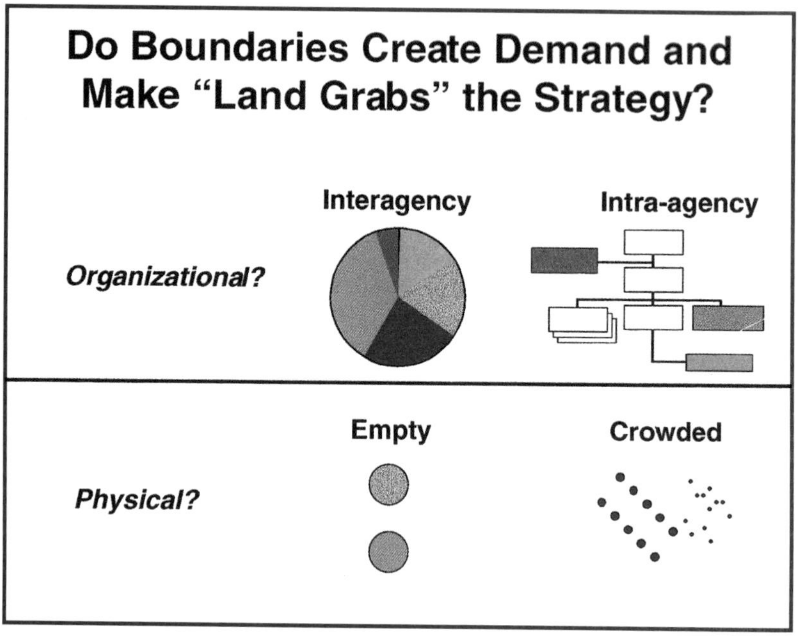

Figure 18

Figure 18 summarizes this section. DoD's land resource is divided by organizational boundaries. These are the different services, major commands, subcommands, and installations. Within each of these are intraorganizational boundaries separating the different functions. The users of the land are separated from the managers. Land management is fragmented among several functional areas.

Installations are individual organizations and are also isolated physical entities. As shown in the bottom of Figure 18, the largest land areas have fewer soldiers and infrastructure than the smaller ones. Large distances separate the small crowded installations from the large parcels.

The title of Figure 18 shows the central questions of this report. Do these boundaries lead to a situation where land is needed locally even if there is aggregate underutilization of the overall Army land resource? Do they also act make "land grabs" or "targets of opportunity" the strategy for addressing this problem?

Chapter Four

LAND REQUIREMENT ASSESSMENT FROM THE INSTALLATION-LEVEL PERSPECTIVE

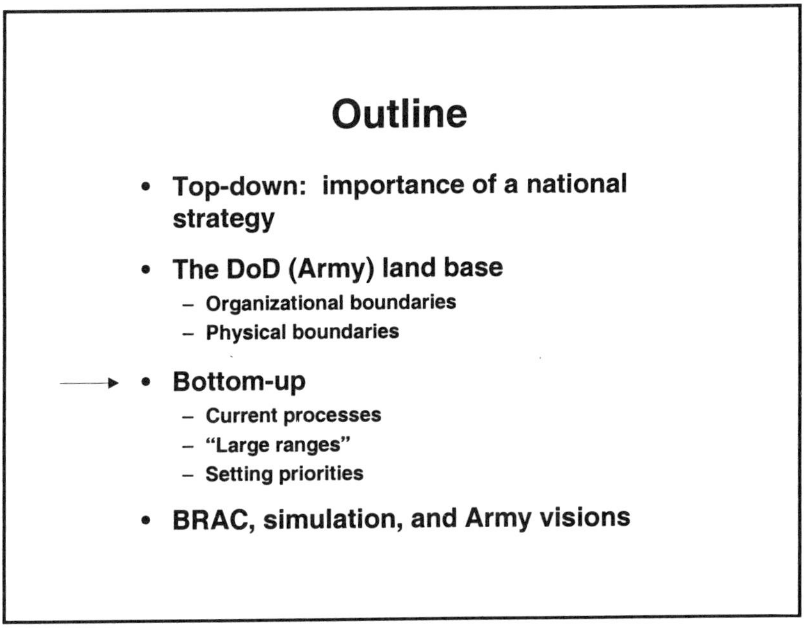

Figure 19

Figure 19 replicates the outline of the briefing and indicates that in this section we will examine the installation-level perspective. First we will review existing processes for establishing land requirements. We will conclude the critic's view of these processes and thus complete the "strawman" argument about Army land policies. We will then consider the physical and organizational obstacles for using the "large ranges" as a reserve of training land and whether it is possible to develop a national priority list of training land initiatives. In general, we will seek to determine how the boundaries described in Figure 18 affect current decisionmaking and future options.

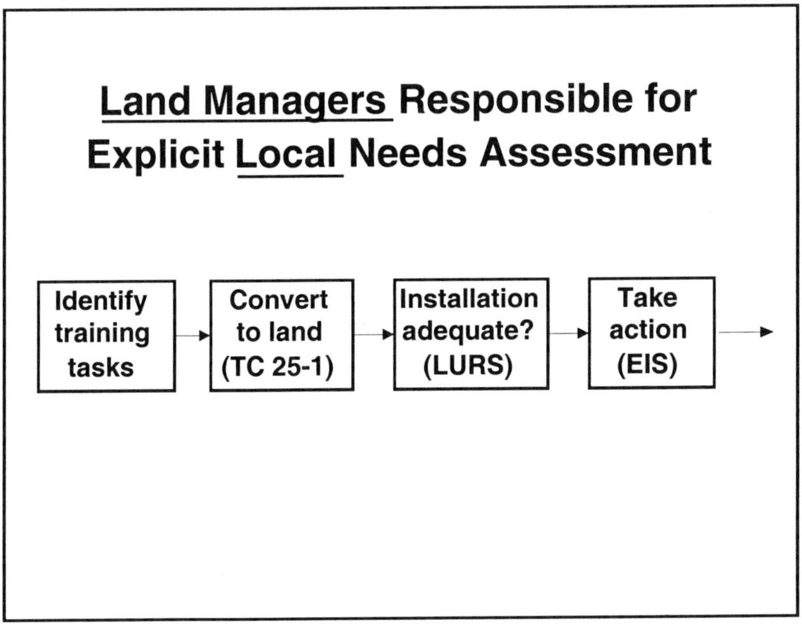

Figure 20

THE LOCAL METHODOLOGY

Figure 20 highlights the Army methodology for analyzing training land requirements. A more detailed flow chart from the governing Army regulation (210-21) is shown in Appendix B.[15] The approach involves an Army-wide methodology employed and interpreted at the local level. Personnel in the Directorate for Plans and Training (DPT) are responsible for implementation. The regulation is written at headquarters and flows to the installations through a "stovepipe" as described in the discussion beneath Figure 17.

The initial step is for range control staff to determine the training tasks that military units will perform at the installation. Army Train-

[15]The process is described in Army Regulation 210-21, *Army Ranges and Training Land Program,* 1 May 1997.

ing Circular (TC) 25-1 specifies the land area required for each training task and how frequently the task must occur. A sample page of information from TC 25-1 is shown in Appendix C.

The third step is to compare the needs with the resources available at the installation. This step is called the Land Use Requirements Study (LURS). The LURS includes an assessment of the installation's land resource along with application of a TC 25-1 methodology describing how to sum land requirements from individual training events to km^2/day. This methodology is known as the Army Training Land Analysis Model (ATLAM). The ATLAM produces two numbers to be compared against the installation's available resource:

1. The size of the largest training event
2. The total land needed to accommodate the sum of all training events in km^2/day

If either number is larger than the installation's resource, the installation should identify compensating actions. AR 210-21 identifies seven specific criteria before a land expansion can be considered.

1. "Decisions must be keyed to a clearly defined study process."
2. "The study process must properly integrate mission and environmental considerations."
3. "All alternatives must be addressed, including improvement of existing internal land management practices."
4. "Justification must be complete, well documented, and analytical. Requirements cannot be based on judgmental factors alone."
5. "All training maneuver area constraints should be reflected in Unit Readiness Reports."
6. "Public participation early in the planning process must be well defined and encouraged."
7. "Annual real property utilization surveys of installations required by AR 405-70 must be completed and kept current."

If these criteria are fulfilled, the installation may initiate an expansion initiative. Most critical is the requirement to include an analysis of alternatives in a well-defined study process.

Any expansion will also require analysis and probably documentation under the National Environmental Policy Act and usually a full Environmental Impact Statement (EIS). The EIS also calls for early public comments and participation.

An important step is the requirement for an installation to review its LURS annually and to "review and update (as necessary)."[16] The first three steps in Figure 20 should be occurring even if an installation is not pursuing a land initiative. We have found that few installations maintain an up-to-date LURS unless there is an ongoing land initiative.

THE ROLE OF HEADQUARTERS

Although the methodology is initiated and interpreted at the local level, higher Army headquarters does maintain an oversight role throughout the process. According to the figure in Appendix B, higher headquarters performs the following oversight roles:

- Major commands review and validate the LURS.
- The Army Staff and the Assistant Secretary of the Army for Installations and Environment (ASA (I&E)) must also approve the LURS.
- The Department of the Army will assign the major command or an external agency the task to conduct an analysis of alternatives.
- The Secretary of the Army must approve the analysis of alternatives and then get permission from the Office of the Secretary of Defense to pursue an expansion.[17]

Headquarters roles emerge from the environmental impact process. Specifically:

---

[16]AR 210-21, Section 1-12.

[17]The Secretary of Defense declared a moratorium on land expansions on September 13, 1990. A special permit is now needed to proceed.

- In virtually all cases, headquarters will need to approve funding for necessary documentation developed under the NEPA.
- Current Army policy requires ASA (I&E) approval for any Notice of Intent involving an EIS.
- There is a similar requirement for any Record of Decision (ROD) made in conjunction with the EIS.

Finally, headquarters will be involved at the end of the process, since a purchase of land will require additional funds. A withdrawal of public land of more than 5,000 acres will require congressional approval. Headquarters will need to work with congressional staff in designing the appropriate legislation.

Despite the significant role of headquarters in providing checks and balances, we conclude that the procedure is primarily a local analysis tool. Consistent Army-wide methods are employed, but the unit of analysis is the local base. An installation's needs are compared against its resources with no consideration of other Army-wide resources. Nevertheless, if the procedures are followed carefully and honestly, the requirement for an analysis of alternatives should offer protection against unnecessary land acquisition. There would be no installation-level "land grabs."

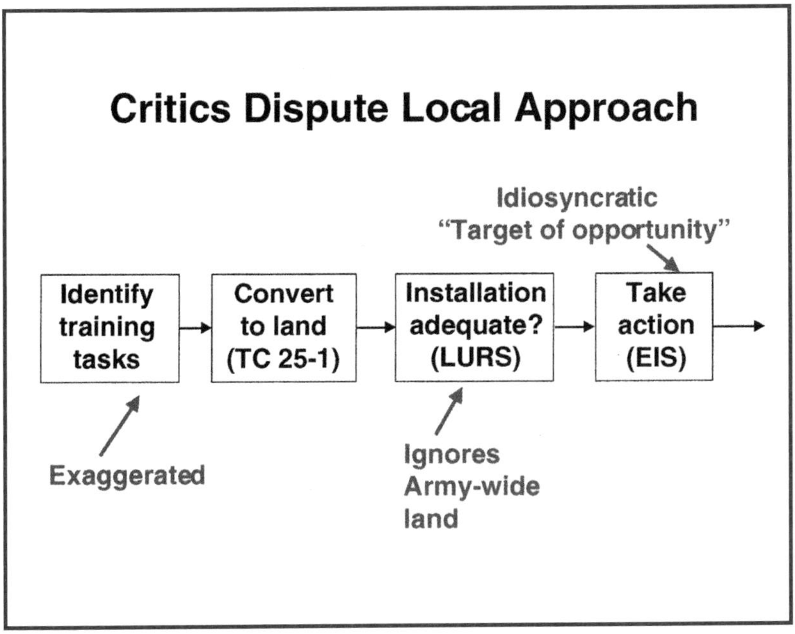

Figure 21

As noted in Figure 8, there have been several critiques of the approach discussed in Figure 20. These are displayed in Figure 21.

The harshest critics argue that the Army is not involved in a fair implementation of its methodology. In this view, the process starts with the last step; the identification of a "target of opportunity" for a "land grab." The installation then exaggerates its requirements to justify a land acquisition.

Even without asserting such motivations, critics claim that the current methodology fails because it does not consider "Army-wide" lands. The LURS process compares installation needs only against installation lands. Installations seek to fulfill their own needs without regard to other Army land initiatives. It follows that a nationwide priority system for land initiatives would eliminate such abuses. Critics also cite the relatively few instances where Army units have formally reported training land as a constraint (step 5 in AR 210-21, as discussed in Figure 20) as further evidence that requirements are exaggerated. Finally, there has been a judgment that the Army does not fairly implement the analysis of alternatives as described in AR 210-21.

The above comments represent a synthesis of several critiques. The following discussion summarizes points made in studies by three agencies that reviewed the methodology.

Army Audit Agency

The Army Audit Agency recently completed a review of Army land acquisition policies and arrived at some of the above conclusions. The work is documented in *Real Estate Acquisitions, Audit Report: AA 98-92,* March 9, 1998. The theme of the report is best summarized by the following citation (p. 15):

> The process used to justify training land acquisitions didn't provide a comprehensive assessment of the Army's total land requirements. Essentially, the process identified training land requirements as the total shortfalls reported at each installation. Because the Army hadn't established its total training land requirements and the capabilities of the land it currently controls, it can't adequately evaluate acquisition requests and set priorities.

The study cites the attempt by three separate installations to justify expansions with the same requirement for armored cavalry reconnaissance. The armored cavalry reconnaissance is significant because it is one of the largest training events specified in TC 25-1.

> It may not be in the best long-term interest of the Army to acquire land at each installation solely to accommodate the largest possible training event of units on that installation. A more prudent approach is to acquire only the land at designated installations to meet Army-wide training land requirements. (p. 16.)

The Audit Agency study also criticizes the Army for not seriously following its own regulations mandating a serious "analysis of alternatives" to expansions. The document argues that these analyses are often conducted after the decision to acquire land has already been reached. It recommends that the Office of the Deputy Chief of Staff for Operations and Plans (ODSCOPS) be given the task of analyzing overall Army-wide land requirements and establishing a priority system for land initiatives.

Army Environmental Policy Institute (AEPI)

AEPI completed a detailed study of Army land management programs in June 1996 titled *Land for Combat Training: A Briefing Book.* Much of the analysis was oriented toward review of existing land management programs rather than the process by which the Army determines land requirements. The study also included a comprehensive description of ways to acquire training land other than through land expansions. These include lease agreements, land exchanges, etc.

The analysis reviewed the methodology described in Figure 20 and the Army approach to acquiring land. AEPI did not criticize the Army for lack of consideration of "Army-wide" lands. It did, however, suggest the need for an Army-wide approach to priority setting, recommending that the Army:

- "Develop a list of priority acquisition needs."
- "Develop a national land acquisition strategy."

AEPI also criticized the use of TC 25-1, stating that the requirements are "optimal areas, not minimums" (p. 51). The study indicated that factors like simulation technology should offset some of the requirements specified in TC 25-1. We will discuss these issues in Figures 24 and 25.

General Accounting Office Studies

The General Accounting Office made the most comprehensive critique of the Army land requirement process in its three studies from the late 1980s and early 1990s (listed in footnote 10, page 24). The studies cast doubt on the need for additional Army lands for the following reasons:

- Land is only one among many factors affecting training and not necessarily the most critical. Land constraints were rarely highlighted on unit status reports (step 5, AR 210-21).
- The Army's most significant training problems were at the individual and small-unit level and hence did not require large blocks of training land.
- Simulations would soon begin to offset the need for training land.
- Units in Europe had access to far less land than units in the United States but reported no adverse impact on training.
- When surveyed, commanders reported highly variable land requirements for similar exercises.

The essence of the GAO argument was that the decision process for land expansions was being made in isolation from the full range of tradeoffs involved in training. The GAO also saw the Army approach to land acquisition as being motivated by "targets of opportunity."[18] Land was being acquired when it was available.

The GAO also criticized the Army's approach to conducting the required analysis of alternatives. It made the same criticism as the Army Audit Agency in noting that the analyses were typically done after a decision to seek land had been taken.[19] The GAO also noted, along with the AAA, that the analyses were conducted at the local level and not with a national perspective.

GAO's recommended alternative was to embed training land in an analysis of all the tools that make up the Army's system for training. This is also a point made by many land managers. Land must be viewed as a training resource that requires proper maintenance and management. GAO recommended that the Army first develop an overall training strategy, with land embedded in that strategy. It could then compare the importance of additional land with other needed training assets.

---

[18]*Army Training: Various Factors Create Uncertainty About Need for More Land*, GAO/NSIAD-91-103, April 1991, p. 41.

[19]*Army Training: Need to Improve the Assessments of Land Requirements and Priorities*, GAO/NSIAD-90-44BR, December 1989, p. 3.

Although this argument contains an inherent logic, the approach has several difficulties. One is that land might be better viewed as a resource that supports a subset of training requirements. Land is generally needed to accomplish maneuver training, and it is difficult to compare its value to time on the gunnery range. A second reason is that the cost of acquiring land is not always comparable to the costs of acquiring other training assets. While most assets require expenditures to acquire, land acquisition may incur political and organizational costs more significant than the financial ones.

Army and DoD Responses

The studies by the Army Audit Agency and the General Accounting Office provided space for the Army and the DoD (in the case of the GAO study) to respond. The general response was to concur with the findings. There was little effort made to highlight problems or inconsistencies in these studies. However, it is not clear that the Army ultimately implemented the recommendations with great vigor.

In response to the GAO study, the DoD concurred with the need to build an overall training strategy that included land as a training resource. The DoD felt that the GAO had not been sufficiently sensitive to the need to conduct higher-echelon training and had overemphasized lower-echelon training. The DoD also felt that while other factors might be more critical in determining readiness, those factors did not reduce the need for additional training lands. The DoD argued that land was not frequently reported as a training problem because after-action reports focus on only those issues the immediate commander can address. Finally, the DoD denied that any expansion proposal was based on the "target of opportunity" rationale.

The Army attached a simple statement to the Army Audit Agency study voicing concurrence with the findings, making only minor comments on minor issues.

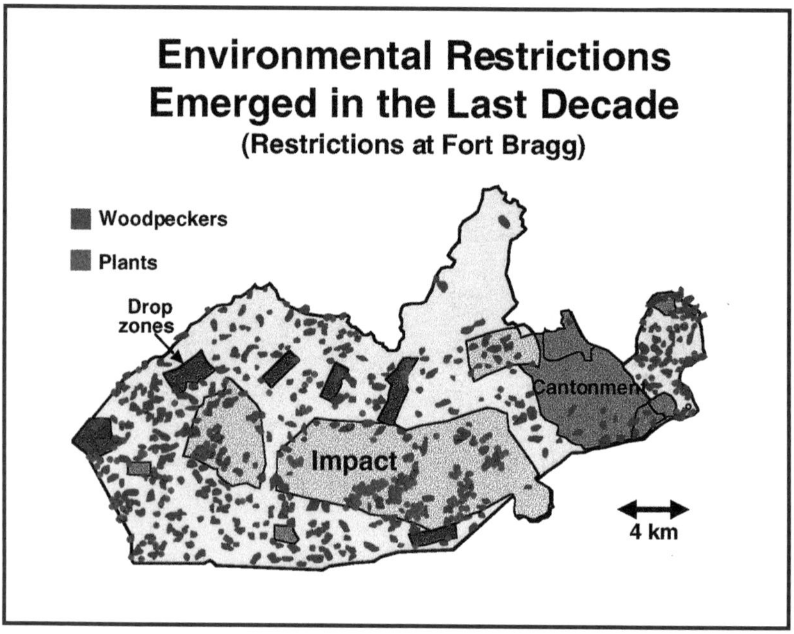

Figure 22a

ENVIRONMENTAL RESTRICTIONS

During the last ten years virtually all installations have had to cope with environmental restrictions on training land use. In addition to partially explaining the need for additional land, environmental restrictions complicate the application of TC 25-1. The latest version of this document was written in 1991 and does not fully recognize environmental issues. This can lead installations to exaggerate training needs to compensate for the apparent inability to account for environmental factors.

Figure 22a shows a graphic example by highlighting the training restricted zones at Fort Bragg arising from requirements for protecting the red-cockaded woodpecker (RCW), which is a listed species under the Endangered Species Act. The so-called "measles" map of Fort Bragg is perhaps the best-known example of training restrictions due to environmental factors. However, since 1992 virtually every other post has been subject to some limitations due to endangered species, wetlands, erosion, or other environmental regulations and concerns.[20]

The red zones in Figure 22a represent RCW buffer zones. These consist of between three and fifteen pine trees where a RCW colony nests, the area within 200 feet of each tree, and the region between them. There are about 300 active (live birds) and 100 inactive (appropriately aged trees without live birds) buffer zones on Fort Bragg. Since 1991 there has been no maneuver through these zones, other than on pre-existing roads. In 1996 the Army and the U.S. Fish and Wildlife Service, the agency responsible for enforcing the Endangered Species Act, agreed to new guidelines for training in the presence of RCW habitat.[21] The new guidelines, which will be implemented at Fort Bragg this year, allow for both wheeled and tracked vehicle transit through the buffer zones, but not within 50 feet of the cavity trees. This breaks up the approximately 400 maneuver-restricted red zones into about 4,000 significantly smaller zones around individual trees. [22]

---

[20]The process leading to the imposition of restrictions at Fort Bragg is described in David Rubenson, Jerome Aroesty, and Charles Thompsen, *Two Shades of Green: Environmental Protection and Combat Training*, Santa Monica, CA: RAND, R-4220-A, 1992. Because of suburban encroachment, Army lands are often the only remnants of older ecosystems and hence contain unusual numbers of endangered species and other ecological values. One assessment concluded that there were more endangered species on military lands than on any of the lands held by the large federal land management agencies. See David Rubenson, Marc Dean Millot, Gwen Farnsworth, and Jerome Aroesty, *More Than 25 Million Acres? DoD as a Federal, Natural, and Cultural Resource Manager*, Santa Monica, CA: RAND, MR-715-OSD, 1996.

[21]See Appendix D for a complete list of the new RCW guideline training restrictions in the buffer zones.

[22]Fort Bragg Range Control informed us that they would be using a 200-foot exclusion zone around each tree even though the broad framework between the Army and the Fish and Wildlife Service allows for 50 feet. Buffer zones with high densities of cavity trees will not be affected, since the current red zone is entirely within 200 feet of a cavity tree. According to range control, about 160 clusters will not be affected. We should also note that Figure 22a shows both active and inactive buffer zones. About a year ago Fish and Wildlife agreed to remove the approximately 100 inactive sites from the restricted area under the condition that approximately 10 sites each year will be added back to account for population growth. If population growth goals are not met, the entire Endangered Species Act process, known as a consultation, could be reopened.

IMPLICATIONS FOR THE TC 25-1 PROCESS

The Fort Bragg LURS

The latest version of TC 25-1 is vague about how installations should treat unusable land. On page 3-5, guidance is given to subtract unusable land due to

- water sites
- environmental restrictions
- encroachment
- shape
- access and availability
- other facilities.

However, the document also states that "acreage figures used in Appendix A [of TC 25-1] to calculate maneuver area requirements include some provision for unusable land. Maneuver units may achieve effective training on smaller areas if ideal terrain is available." This implies some unusable land has already been accounted for.

The vagueness leaves discretion to the installations on how to calculate total training land. Figure 22b illustrates how Fort Bragg interpreted the Training Circular in its recent LURS used to support the expansion mentioned in Figure 7.

The left half of Figure 22b shows the division of Fort Bragg's 144,000 acres. After subtracting for cantonment, environmental restricted zones (largely the red buffer zones), and impact areas, there are only 66,384 acres available for maneuver.

The right half of Figure 22b compares this maneuver area with doctrinal requirements from TC 25-1. The figure shows that the 66,384 acres are suitable for a light infantry battalion maneuver but not for armored cavalry squadron reconnaissance. 66,384 acres is also large enough for armored battalion maneuver.

At the time of the LURS study, the 82nd Airborne at Fort Bragg contained the 3-73 Armor Battalion. That unit is no longer at Fort Bragg,

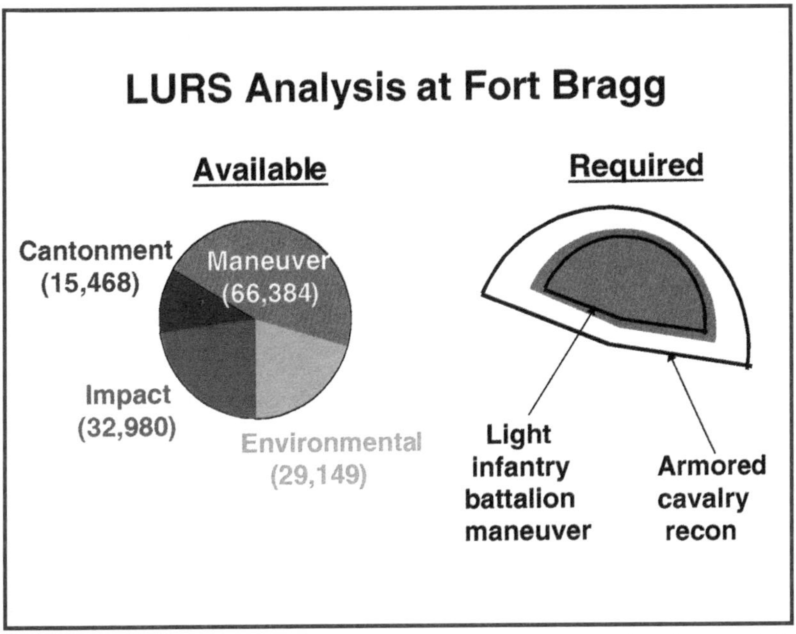

Data taken from *Land-Use Requirements Study, Fort Bragg, North Carolina,* May 1995.

Figure 22b

leading to uncertainty about the need for the reconnaissance mission and perhaps lending some validity to the Army Audit Agency conclusion that this maneuver is invoked too frequently. However, the LURS study only excluded 29,149 acres for environmental restrictions, even though the fragmentation at Fort Bragg reduces the training value of almost all of the land.

Rather than choose the armored cavalry maneuver, Fort Bragg could have justified the expansion by eliminating significantly more acreage from the total of usable maneuver area.[23] In this case, an expansion would have been motivated by a significantly smaller

[23]We should note that the Fort Bragg LURS showed a land deficit for both the largest training event and the sum total of all events. The LURS reported a need for 76,360,826 acre-days and a supply of 21,906,720.

training event. TC 25-1 calls for excluding land due to shape constraints for "irregular post outlines and noncontiguous parcels that prevent movement or channelize forces." The limitations at Bragg are, in the narrowest sense, not the result of noncontiguous parcels or irregular post outlines, though they do result in the need to channelize forces. By taking this narrow interpretation, only the largest of training events can highlight the limitations imposed by environmental restrictions.

Invoking Large Training Events

As noted in the discussion beneath Figure 21, one criticism of the Army's methodology is that TC 25-1 exaggerates acreage requirements for individual training events. A second criticism is that installations exaggerate the type of training events to justify expansions driven by "targets of opportunity." The Fort Bragg LURS illustrates a case where TC 25-1 did not motivate the installation to aggressively subtract out land that could not sustain maneuver. Instead the installation invoked a large training event as an alternative. However, the broader picture is that environmental restrictions have left Fort Bragg critically short of training land along with insufficient land to manage the RCW. If Fort Bragg's use of the large armored cavalry reconnaissance maneuver represented an exaggeration, it compensated for the TC 25-1 lack of specificity with regard to environmental constraints. It led to an appropriate assessment of installation needs.

OTHER FORCES COMMAND HOME STATIONS

As mentioned above, most military bases are now subject to environmental restrictions that affect training to varying degrees. Figure 22c shows the effects of restrictions on the ability to do heavy unit training at Fort Lewis, the home of the 3rd Armored Division.

The figure shows that in addition to facilities and impact areas, environmental restrictions significantly reduce the area available for maneuver training. In addition to sensitive areas, much of Fort Lewis is too heavily wooded for maneuver. In the past these areas might have been cleared, but the base was declared critical habitat for the spotted owl in the 1990s. Although there are no owls on Fort Lewis, and the trees are probably too young for the birds, the base is managed

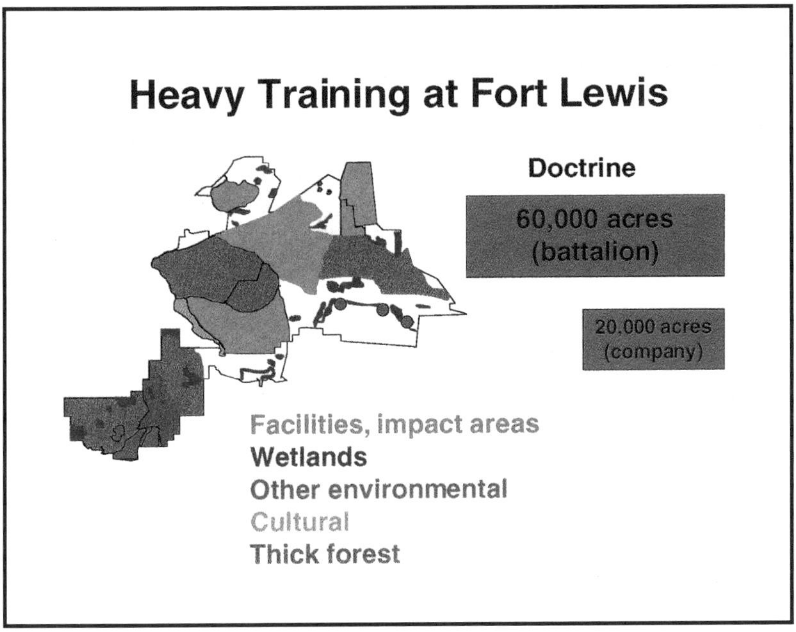

Figure 22c

with the long-term goal of creating owl habitat. This prevents any efforts to clear a significant number of trees to create maneuver land.

The result of these restrictions is that Fort Lewis is extremely constrained for heavy unit maneuver. As shown in Figure 22c, even company maneuvers cannot be conducted in a manner consistent with doctrine (as described in TC 25-1).

Figure 22d shows that even at Fort Hood, which is often viewed as the Army's premier home station for active units, there are environmental issues that affect training.

As seen in Figure 22d, it is difficult to lay down a TC 25-1 armored battalion maneuver box on the installation without crossing some areas of environmental concern or areas where terrain conditions prevent maneuver training.

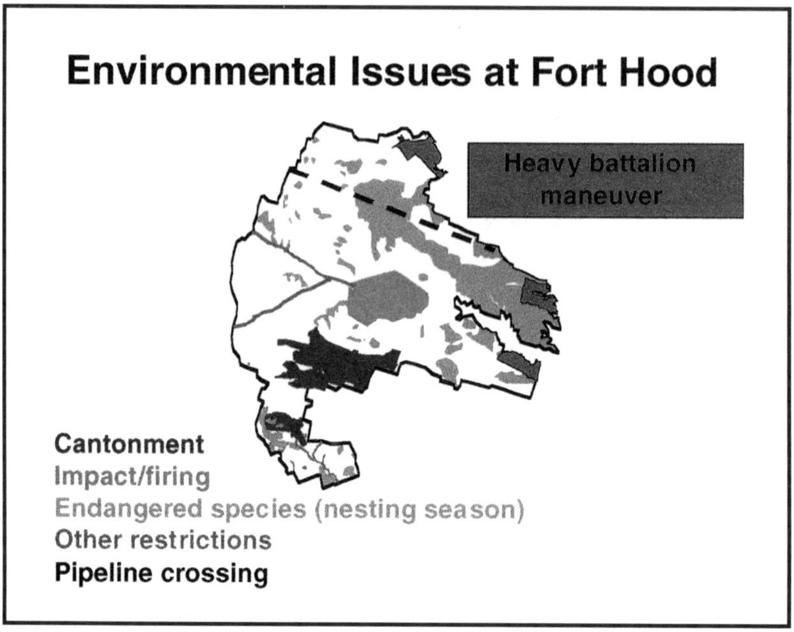

SOURCE: Fort Hood Range Control Office.

Figure 22d

A LONG-TERM SUSTAINABILITY CONSTRAINT?

One concern of the Army environmental community has been the long-term carrying capacity or sustainability of Army lands. The Army's Integrated Training Area Management (ITAM) program has been monitoring the status of vegetative cover on Army installations for more than a decade. Much of this information has been gained by detailed randomized plot samples, taken at intervals long enough to determine trends.

Vegetative cover is not by itself a parameter often monitored by environmental regulators and does not directly lead to the type of restrictions highlighted in Figure 22a. It can, however, be an indicator of long-term problems that ultimately lead to direct intervention by regulators. Natural resource issues that can lead to regulatory intervention include Clean Water Act issues, fugitive dust, or degradation of habitat needed by endangered species. However, Fort Irwin is an example of an installation that, due to intensive training and highly erodable soils, is far from retaining a sustainable level of vegetative cover. Nevertheless it remains a premier place to conduct training. But it can be argued that significant habitat destruction had occurred before concern arose about issues like the desert tortoise, which is now listed as a threatened species under the Endangered Species Act. It is unlikely that the habitat destruction that occurred in the past on Fort Irwin would be allowed today.

The Center for Ecological Management of Military Lands (CEMML) at Colorado State University designed many of the protocols for the ITAM program and staffs many of the field offices conducting land surveys. In 1996, CEMML produced a national survey related to the sustainability of Army installations.[24] Similar to the LURS process, the two factors in the assessment are sustainability of the resource and the level of use. While accurate usage data (such as tracked vehicle miles per year) is scarce, the study did review trends in environmental observations that led to the conclusion that Army lands are not sustainable at current use rates. The implication is that an increasingly greater fraction of Army lands will have to be removed from use to allow for rest and recovery.

The Army is currently continuing CEMML's efforts to analyze the sustainability issue by refining the concept of carrying capacity. The Army Training and Testing Area Carrying Capacity (ATACC) model is aimed at linking the usage at an installation to the effects on ground cover. In this way degradation can be predicted and revenues for restoration properly targeted. Installations where restoration provides significant benefits would receive more funds than installations where restoration is unneeded or impossible to accomplish. One significant challenge is to build a model that is sufficiently accurate to compare degradation effects and restoration needs at installations with vastly different types of soil and vegetation. Such comparison is needed if the model is to be used to predict the most effective method of spending the limited funds dedicated to soil restoration.

---

[24]Robert Shaw and David Kowalski, *U.S. Army Lands: A National Survey*, CEMML TPS 96-1, Colorado State University, March 1996.

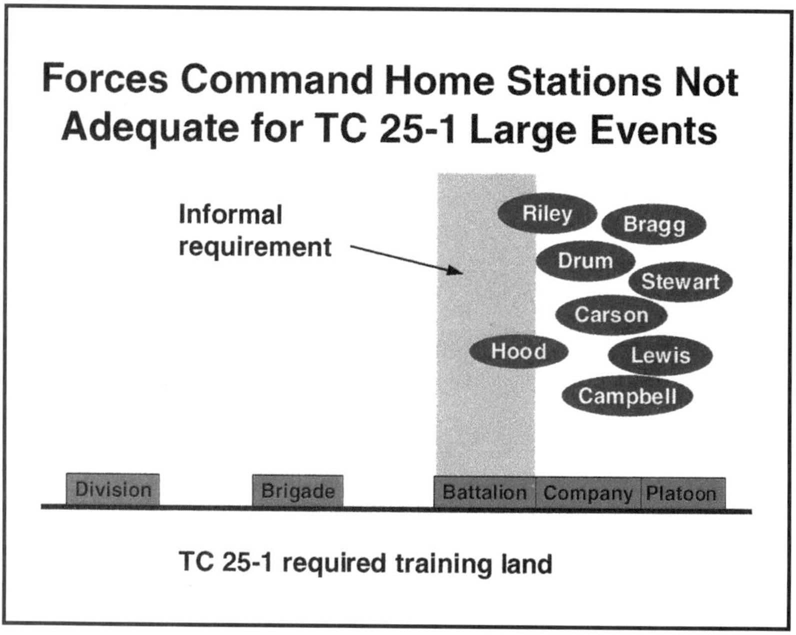

Figure 23

SINGLE LARGE TRAINING EVENT

Figure 23 makes a rough placement of the Forces Command home station maneuver areas along a scale of military activity designated by TC 25-1. *The figure represents the laydown of TC 25-1 maneuver boxes over terrain, not the actual training done at these installations.* There are credible arguments that TC 25-1 is not a good measure of training land needs and that the laydown of these boxes over realistic terrain requires subjective judgments. By stating that installations are "not adequate for TC 25-1 large events," we mean that it is not possible to overlay a TC 25-1 maneuver box over land free of major environmental or terrain restrictions. The figure mixes heavy and light training that have similar maneuver area requirements, though the former is typically subject to more environmental constraints.[25] Forts Campbell, Bragg, and Drum emphasize light unit maneuver, whereas the others are the homes for heavy units.

What size maneuver box should a home station be able to accommodate? Major Forces Command home stations are commanded by division or corps commanders and typically house a single division. The Army works on a system where the commander at a particular level will plan, resource, and monitor activities of units two levels beneath his own. A division commander will monitor the planning of battalion-level activities and will receive performance reports of battalions and brigades. A corps commander will plan and resource for brigade-level training and receive performance reports at the brigade and division level, but typically not the battalion level. Since some Forces Command home stations often house full divisions, it is desirable for these home stations to accommodate full battalion-level training. This informal requirement is highlighted in Figure 23.

The organizational level that should be supported in field training is only tenuously tied to the "two levels below the commander" paradigm. It is desirable for home stations only housing brigades to also have battalion-level training facilities. There is a broad consensus in the Army that battalion commanders must go to the field with their battalions so that they can learn to fight as battalions. There is a less frequent need to train at the brigade level. If an installation can support battalion-level training, there will be little pressure for expansion.

As discussed below Figure 22b, there is no detailed method of accounting for unusable terrain in determining whether an installation can support a given training exercise. As shown in Figure 22d, even Fort Hood, often described as the Army's most expansive home station, cannot accommodate the 8 × 31-kilometer maneuver box without crossing endangered species habitat or areas where other restrictions occur. As illustrated in Figure 22c, it is difficult to accommodate full company-level training at Fort Lewis.

---

[25]TC 25-1 lists "movement to contact" for a heavy infantry or armored battalion is listed as 8 × 31 km or 248 km^2. In contrast, "movement to contact" for a light infantry battalion is listed as 19 × 14 km or 266 km^2.

Several installations referenced in Figure 23 were not discussed in Figure 22. Fort Stewart has 279,000 acres and is Forces Command's largest home station. But the swampy terrain divides the post into narrow lanes suitable for platoon-level or at best company-level maneuver. On the opposite scale is Fort Riley, which at 100,000 acres is one of the smallest home stations. But it has few environmental or terrain restrictions, and there is a fairly wide open 6 × 17-kilometer rectangular maneuver box running north-south through the installation. The major restriction is a busy highway running through the middle of the box in a north-south direction. Units must make administrative crossings to utilize the full 5–6 kilometers of width.

MULTIPLE SMALLER EVENTS

Figure 23 compares the open land at installations with the doctrinal requirements for single large maneuver events. Installations may also be short of land because of a high frequency of smaller exercises. The recent *Installation Training Capacity* (ITC) study measured installation size with this metric and arrived at the results in the table on the next page. The percentages refer to the fraction of maneuver land available at an installation relative to what is needed. *It is important to emphasize that the ITC study assumed all units would have adequate funding to conduct all required training.* Currently, Army training levels are well below requirements due to budget constraints.

With the exception of the two home stations (Lewis and Carson) that were combined with regional training centers, the ITC results based on cumulative use yield the same conclusion as the large training event formulation in Figure 23: few home stations have adequate land resources. The most notable distinction is Fort Hood, which can almost accommodate a battalion-level maneuver but has more difficulty accommodating the diverse and numerous smaller training activities of its two armored divisions. The table shows that Fort Hood has only 18 percent of the needed land. Fort Hood is large, but overcrowded.

Installation	Percent of Required Land
Hood	18%
Campbell	33%
Bragg	35%
Riley	35%
Drum	37%
Stewart	81%
Polk	135%
Lewis/Yakima[a]	206%
Carson/Piñon[a]	215%

NOTE: Percentages are the TC 25-1 fraction of required land available (assumes full funding of training).

[a]The ITC study combined Fort Lewis and Fort Carson with regional training centers and made a joint assessment as if the separated facilities constituted a single installation. We will discuss these combinations later in the text.

OTHER INSTALLATIONS

The patterns for many other "home stations" of the major commands will be similar to that for Forces Command. Most TRADOC bases are undersized given the range of new weapons. Even the White Sands Missile Range (WSMR), with 2 million acres and a declining level of activity, is involved in tests with systems of increasingly longer range. WSMR has negotiated arrangements for evacuation of areas outside the base and recently went through a protracted environmental process to obtain rights to launch missiles from off post.

There are obviously bases where additional land would provide few benefits. There are also cases where the Army would prefer to close bases, and realign the units, rather than expend the resources to make them viable through land expansion and other upgrades. But until there is another BRAC round, the above conclusions will be relevant for much of the Army.

TRAINED AND READY?

Despite the gap between doctrinal needs and available land, few units cite land shortages as a readiness problem. This was a central critique in the GAO report referenced earlier.

At the current time, problems related to land shortages are insignificant compared to budgetary constraints. The Army would like active armor units to achieve 800 operational tempo (OPTEMPO) miles each year. Units are now getting about half that total. The recent FY99 budget agreement allocated almost 9 billion additional dollars to the DoD, primarily for the purposes of increasing readiness.

Until OPTEMPO budgets increase, the land shortages in Figure 23 will remain a relatively small problem. However, it is not just funding constraints that mask the issue of land requirements. As will be seen in the next figure, TC 25-1 does not fully reflect Army land requirements. Instead it reflects a regulation written for the range control function that does not account for other compensating activities at an Army post.

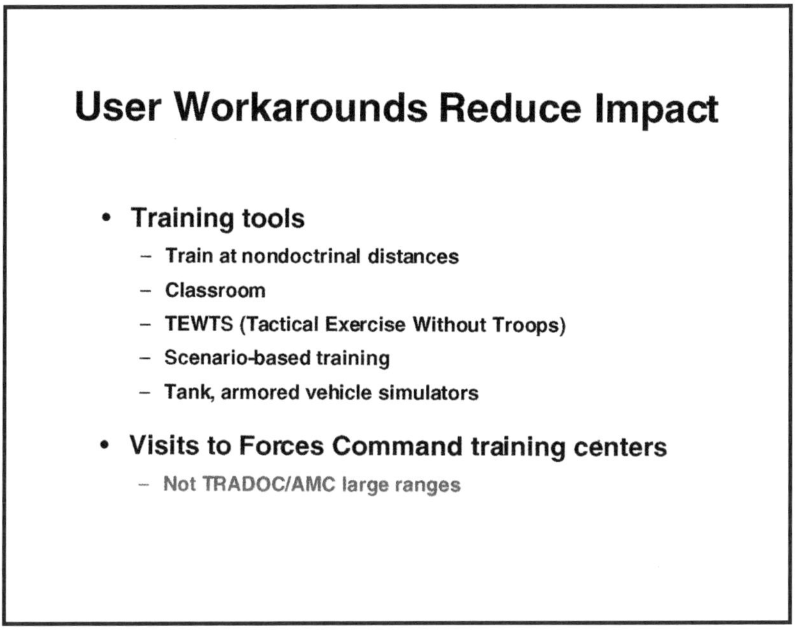

Figure 24

Figure 24 lists techniques Army units use to compensate for land shortages. These are not reflected in the TC 25-1 methodology. The training units (the land users) implement these techniques, whereas the Directorate of Plans and Training (one of the land managers) is responsible for TC 25-1. In other words, intraorganizational boundaries (Figure 17) lead to a methodology that does not reflect the complete set of factors comprising land requirements.

TRAINING TOOLS

A variety of techniques are at the disposal of local commanders to overcome deficits in home station training land. One approach is to conduct classroom sessions to discuss the distinction between space-constrained exercises and actual battlefield conditions. This is primarily done with officers.

TEWTS, or Tactical Exercises Without Troops, are exercises conducted primarily by officers and other leaders in wheeled vehicles. Personnel move over terrain in a manner similar to that of a large maneuver but only for the purposes of exercising planning and communications. TEWTS can occur both on post or off post, as they have almost no impact on the land or ecology.

Units will also conduct scenario-based or "as-if" training. Virtually every Army training exercise is built around a battle scenario designed to practice one of the tasks on a unit's Mission Essential Task List (METL). In scenario-based training, to compensate for a lack of land, units will maneuver as if they were engaged in a larger exercise and behave as if other forces (friendly or enemy) were deployed beyond the boundaries of the installation. For example, Fort Stewart has two narrow parallel maneuver lanes that can accommodate platoons, but the exercise can take place at a simulated battalion level. The maneuvering platoons act as if friendly units are moving alongside the two lanes. The actual platoons then conduct activities as if they were the spearhead for a full battalion attack. While such training is not optimal, it does allow units to practice the techniques that might be needed in combat.

SIMULATION

For more than a decade the Army has pursued the development of diverse technologies in the hope that some fraction of training activities could be conducted in a simulated environment. The primary motivation has been the potentially lower cost of simulated training compared to actual field exercises. The indirect impact on land requirements has been given less attention and is poorly understood.

Today's Army uses simulation for command and staff exercises and is initiating its use for small-unit training. As will be discussed in Figure 37, an ambitious research agenda may increase simulation's scope and effectiveness in the future. However, the pace of development, and the implications for training, have not been as dramatic as indicated in the above-referenced GAO studies of the early 1990s.

Simulation for Command and Staff Exercises

The primary use of simulation during the past decade has been for wargaming. Several legacy simulations like JANUS, the Brigade Battalion Simulation (BBS), and the Corps Battle Simulation (CBS) have been used mainly for command and staff training. Because of their Cold War heritage, these simulations focus on two-sided wargames with traditional land combat scenarios. They typically do not capture joint and coalition operations, peacekeeping, or operations other than war. They are pure, or constructive, simulations in that they operate without a man in the loop.

Effectively representing and employing assets from other services (e.g., for close air support) or coalition forces requires the ability to integrate distinct simulations. The recent advent of SIMNET, the prototype of networked, man-in-the-loop simulations, and the establishment of standard Distributed Interactive Simulation (DIS) protocols for linking simulations have advanced the design of future constructive simulations in ways that will increase their richness.

Simulated Live Fire

Laser engagement systems are currently used to simulate live fire to allow a BLUEFOR (friendly forces) to train safely against a live OPFOR (opposing force). These laser engagement systems consist of kits installed on tanks and armored personnel carriers that maneuver over real terrain in the course of a training exercise. Laser engagement systems and other information technologies have enabled the Army to develop the NTC into the world's premier training center for land combat forces.

Armored and Mechanized Vehicle Simulators

Perhaps the most significant development for training land has been the advent of fighting vehicle simulators. The Close Combat Tactical Trainer (CCTT) is the first of the Combined Arms Tactical Trainers (CATT) the Army expects to develop. It will enable the Army to drill individuals and crews and to train for platoon, company, and potentially battalion tactics. The CCTT provides not only the crew stations, but also the communications with the Tactical Operations Center

(TOC) mockup for command and control, and the terrain of the simulated battlefield in which the unit operates. This conveys the illusion of operating the actual vehicle.

Computer-generated forces created by the CCTT SAF (Semi-Automated Forces) simulate both an OPFOR and additional friendly units to provide a complete scenario. As a result, the efficacy of the simulated experience of CCTT appears to be quite good. With CCTT, units can train for most of the tasks of an armored platoon or company/team. On the other hand, there appears to be almost unanimous sentiment among members of the EXFOR (experimental force) who have used it at Fort Hood that it prepares a unit to train in the field but does not actually replace field training. Nevertheless, units can probably reach a particular level of proficiency with less time spent in the field by training with the CCTT. However, the efficacy of the simulated experience, as compared to field exercises, has not been documented and there is a lively debate within the Army about the realism and utility of the CCTT exercises. To date, the EXFOR unit at Fort Hood is the only unit with substantial (6 months) experience using the CCTT. Within the next two years or so, the fielding of 11 fixed sites for active forces and 21 mobile units will be completed. This should lead to a better understanding of the extent to which simulations can actually reduce the frequency of field training exercises.

TRAINING CENTERS

Forces Command home station units also utilize the Forces Command training centers (Figure 14) to provide opportunities to train on larger parcels. Visits are primarily limited to once every other year for the NTC or the JRTC depending on whether the unit is heavy or light. Fort Lewis units conduct temporary training at Yakima approximately twice a year, and the 3rd Armored Cavalry Regiment (ACR) has made three visits to Piñon Canyon in the two years it has been based at Fort Carson.

Visits to NTC and JRTC provide numerous benefits in addition to the opportunity to train on larger parcels. There is a well-trained OPFOR, technologies that support simulated engagement, and the opportunity to review exercises and compare results with other units.

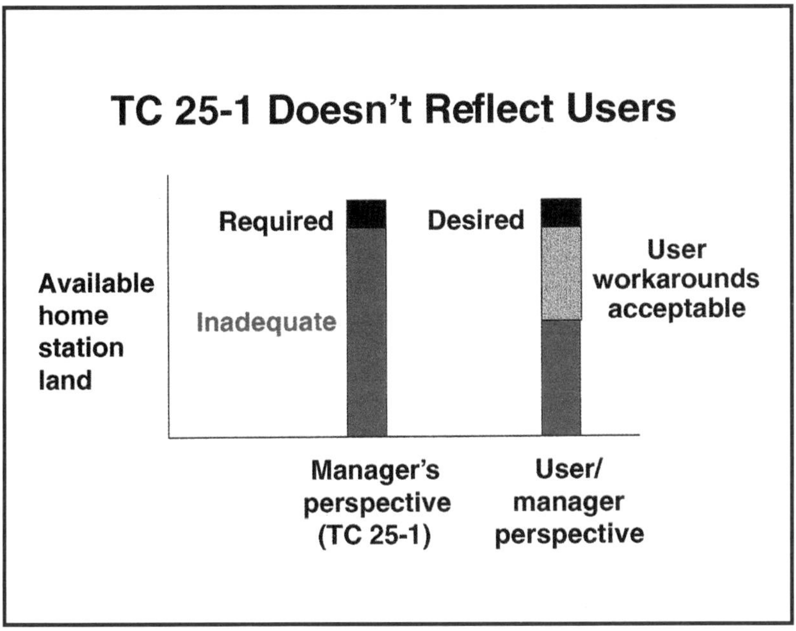

Figure 25

Figure 25 places the use of TC 25-1 in the context of the "workarounds" discussed in Figure 24.

The left side of Figure 25 shows the application of TC 25-1 without considering the techniques described in Figure 24. It leads to the conclusions that home stations have insufficient land and that readiness will suffer.

The right side of Figure 25 displays a use of TC 25-1 that accounts for the techniques in Figure 24. It illustrates the satisfactory but not optimal conditions made possible by the workarounds. Few home station installations meet TC 25-1 requirements, but most have sufficient land to train satisfactorily. There is a "gray area" of installations that would benefit from additional land but do not absolutely require it. Obviously there is a point where limitations become so severe that workarounds are not sufficient. While few, if any, home stations are at this point, a continued increase in battlespace could lead to that result.[26]

These conclusions are in partial agreement with the GAO reports that recommended making land part of a national training strategy. GAO recommended that the cost of new land be compared with alternative investments that enhance training. Our conclusion highlights the distinctions among installations and the difficulty of arriving at a single formula. It is more realistic to include land needs within the context of an overall installation training strategy.

---

[26]See *Defense Daily*, October 28, 1998, p. 6, for statements of concern from senior military leadership about the adequacy of existing range space for meeting future needs.

Do "Home Stations" Need Land?

- Physical boundaries create needs "everywhere"
- TC 25-1 documents needs
- Organizational boundaries exaggerate them, by masking implicit strategy
  - Workarounds
  - Training centers
- Can further use of "large ranges" offset expansion needs?

Figure 26

Figure 26 summarizes the status of Forces Command "home stations" and the Army's current methodology for determining land requirements.

Home stations are arguably the Army's most important installations because they house trained and ready-to-fight units. They are of only moderate size and are physically isolated from the "training centers" and "large ranges." They are not adequately sized to meet doctrinally specified requirements in Army Training Circular 25-1. 25-1 could justify expansion at any Forces Command home station.

Although all home stations would benefit from additional land, TC 25-1 exaggerates the need. Implemented by the range control function, it does not include techniques employed by the users to minimize the adverse effects of shortfalls of training land. These include a variety of training techniques and visits to Forces Command "training centers."

The use of Forces Command "training centers" suggests that additional land shortages might be offset by use of the "large ranges." The fact that they are not used in this manner suggests that organizational boundaries might be preventing the Army from employing this practice. We will discuss this possibility in the next several charts.

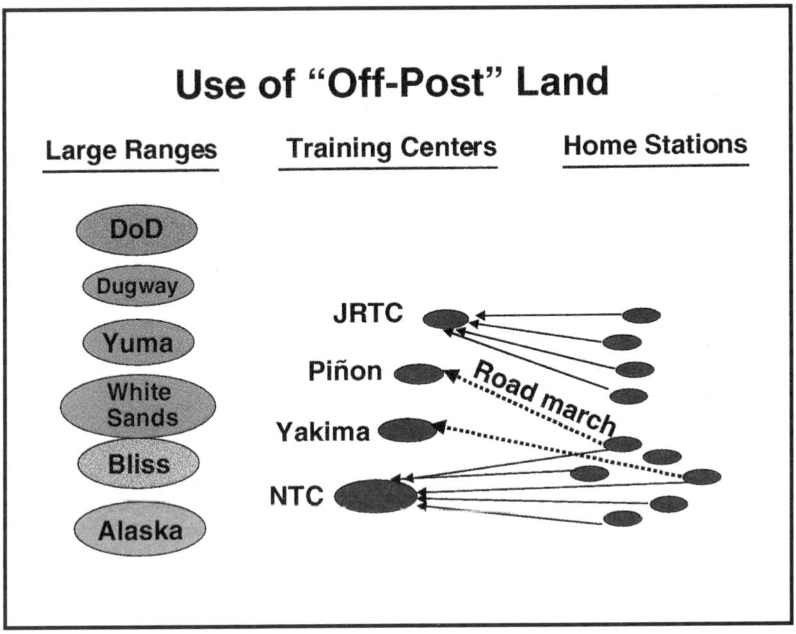

Figure 27

Figure 27 shows a schematic of the temporary training discussed in Figure 24. This training is used to help overcome "home station" shortfalls. As indicated by the color code, Forces Command home stations use Forces Command "training centers." The "large ranges" are decoupled from the training portion of the Army.[27] This suggests that the "large ranges" might be used as an alternative to land expansion. It also suggests that organizational boundaries are preventing an efficient use of the Army land resource.

[27]Fort Bliss does house the Forces Command air defense units at corps level and above. Its large land resources are not used by other active units.

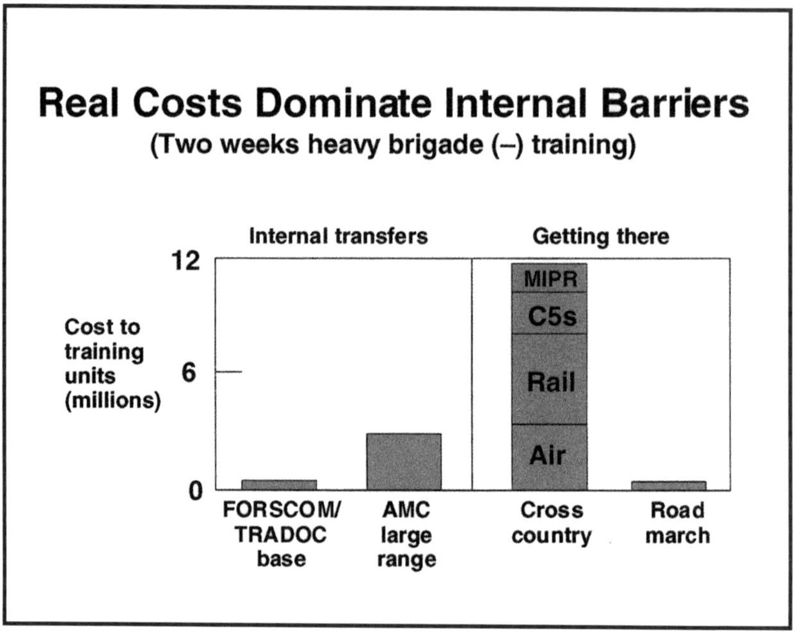

Figure 28

Figure 28 compares the organizational and physical obstacles for using "large ranges" for temporary training. It suggests that although organizational boundaries are important, physical distances are the primary problem.

The right half of Figure 28 shows the costs to move a heavy brigade (–) for two weeks of temporary training across the country. A heavy brigade (–) consists of two battalions and brigade-level units and support. Costs include air charter for troops, rail costs for equipment, MIPR for miscellaneous travel expenses, and the costs of moving helicopters on C-5 aircraft. Prepositioning of heavy equipment would lower rail costs by approximately 65 percent.[28] If distances are short (less than 200 miles), road marching of light vehicles

---

[28]Transport costs were derived from Forces Command budgets for moving units to the NTC, inputs from U.S. Transportation Command, and data on deployment costs for units moving from Fort Carson to Piñon Canyon.

and troops combined with prepositioning can dramatically reduce costs. Costs to move units less than cross-country distances (but longer than road marches) vary with distance. Thus, the cost of moving a unit from Fort Riley to NTC, where heavy equipment is prepositioned, is about $4–5 million.

The left half of Figure 28 shows the internal financial transfers required for a visiting unit to utilize a range. Costs to utilize a Forces Command or TRADOC installation may consist of mess fees and a nominal range fee. Fort Bliss is the only TRADOC installation to qualify as a "large range," and there are no such Forces Command posts. Costs to access an AMC test range are significantly higher and include some of the fixed operating costs of a sophisticated test range. Test ranges (AMC) recover all fixed operating costs from users, while training ranges (TRADOC and Forces Command) receive appropriated operating budgets. This means that training units never see the funds used to operate their home stations. However, the price of using test ranges includes fixed operating costs that can be prohibitively expensive for trainers.

The costs shown in the left half of Figure 28 are for two weeks of training at White Sands Missile Range.[29] Though large, this value is small compared to paying the costs for the long movements to White Sands (see Figure 16b). It would be very difficult to road march to White Sands from even the closest of Forces Command home stations.

The importance of transport costs was demonstrated by III Corps artillery's recent decision to abandon a longstanding practice of using Fort Bliss for temporary training. III Corps typically sent nine MLRS and three Paladin battalions from Fort Sill to Bliss for their annual external evaluation. Rail costs were approximately $135,000 per

---

[29]The numbers are based on the $15,000/hour that White Sands charged the Roving Sands training exercise at Fort Bliss for use of the entire White Sands airspace. White Sands claims that this precludes use by test customers. We assumed that a large training exercise would use 10 percent of White Sands and cost 10 percent of the fee. Since White Sands charges fees based on the instrumentation used (or precluded from use by the training activity) and not the land used, the number in Figure 27 is a rough approximation. White Sands does not have an established fee structure for use of land without corresponding use of instrumentation.

battalion.[30] Bliss's large distances allow significantly more flexibility for firing MLRS. Fort Bliss is a TRADOC installation, so III Corps can use it without paying for its fixed operating costs.

The multimillion-dollar costs in Figure 28 are significant in today's Army budget. The Army's 10 divisions receive approximately $1.1 billion,[31] leaving about $35 million for each brigade. The costs in Figure 28 are for movement of a brigade (–), hence to move the entire brigade (across the country) would require roughly 150 percent of these costs. Assuming a movement across half the country (about $4 to $5 million for a brigade (–)), a single cross-country move might represent about 25 percent of a full brigade's annual resources. If heavy equipment was already prepositioned at the training site, then total costs would be reduced by about 20 percent but would still remain a significant part of a brigade's budget for a single exercise. While costs of units at Fort Hood to use Fort Bliss might even be lower (approximately half the amount), such expenditure is not practical for routine recurring training.

In addition to financial costs, movement across country for temporary training is time consuming. Packing, loading, transport, check-out of prepositioned equipment, the actual training, check-in, reloading, and transport back home require about seven weeks for an NTC rotation. The decision to deploy for temporary training must balance the training benefits against the costs and the lost time.

---

[30]Communication from the G3 Training at III Corps.

[31]Department of the Army, Assistant Secretary of the Army for Financial Management, *The Army Budget,* April 1998. An additional $300 million is provided for training of units at corps level and above.

Temporary Training at Centers or Large Ranges

- Obstacles using “large ranges”
  - Organizational
  - More important physical distances
- Two “training centers” within road march
- NTC/JRTC provide multiple benefits:
  - Large land area
  - OPFOR
  - Instrumentation
  - Replay capability

“Large ranges” can’t offset land shortages today

Figure 29

Figure 29 summarizes the preceding discussion of using large land parcels for temporary training. It explains why movements to NTC are affordable while similar-distance movements to “large ranges” are not.

Figure 28 indicated that costs to move units are more significant than internal institutional obstacles. Forts Lewis and Carson do use Yakima and Piñon Canyon because those centers are within road march distance of the home stations.

Costs to visit NTC are significantly higher because it is far from home stations. If land were the only reason for visiting NTC, it is unlikely that the Army or individual commanders would choose to go. However, NTC (and JRTC) offer numerous training benefits that amortize the costs of the visits. Both centers offer a well-trained opposing force (OPFOR), expert observers and controllers, an instrumentation system that allows for simulated battles, and the capability to replay exercises for diagnostics and learning. These and other factors, of which land is only one, make the National Training Center the world's most effective training facility for ground forces.

We conclude that under today's budgets, "large ranges" cannot offset Army training land needs. Financial limitations confine units to home stations with the exception of a visit to NTC every other year. Home stations are effectively isolated and must either use "work-arounds" to cope with training land shortfalls or seek expansion.

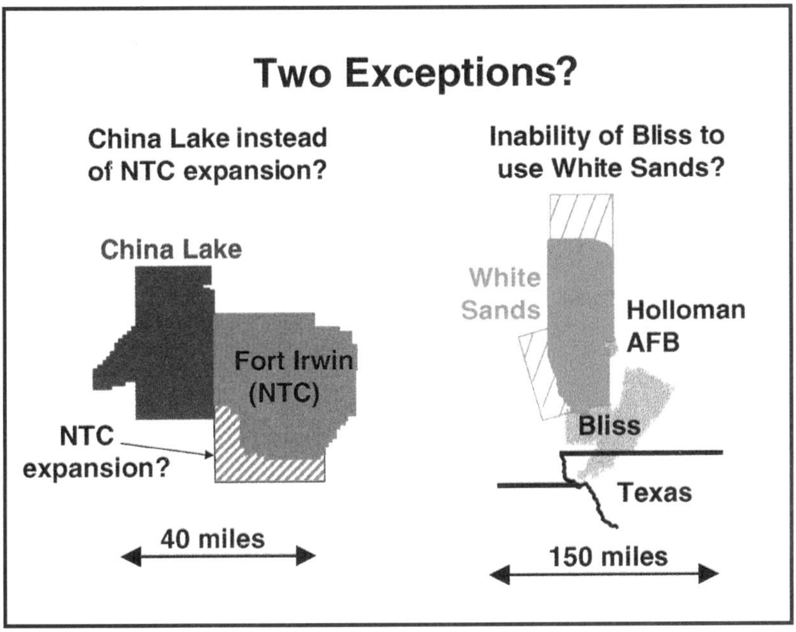

Figure 30

In Figure 29 we concluded that the physical distances between "home stations" and "large ranges" prevent the routine use of "Army-wide" lands to offset "home station" land shortages. The cost of moving units is a larger obstacle than internal DoD or Army organizational boundaries.

Figure 30 shows two possible exceptions. As will be discussed in Figures 32 and 33, Fort Irwin has been attempting to expand southward for almost 15 years. There has been little serious consideration of the use of China Lake Naval Test Center as an alternative. Much of the reason is the test community's view that the training and test missions are incompatible. The different financial structures and the corresponding inability of trainers to pay for access to a test range also dissuade China Lake from seeking training activity. Nevertheless, China Lake has declining activity and is adjacent to Fort Irwin.

Another example has been the failure to achieve efficient joint use of Fort Bliss and the White Sands Missile Range. Fort Bliss hosts an annual joint and international air defense exercise called Roving Sands. Although Bliss contains 1.2 million acres, the scope of Roving Sands is so large that the exercise would benefit from easy access to White Sands. However, White Sands charges approximately $15,000/hour for use of its airspace. This charge is due largely to the differing financial structures discussed in Figure 28. White Sands suffers from declining activity levels, and the prices it charges have been rising in order to recover fixed costs from a declining customer base.

Outline

- Top-down: importance of a national strategy
- The DoD (Army) land base
  - Organizational boundaries
  - Physical boundaries
- Bottom-up
  - Current processes
  - "Large ranges"
  - → Setting priorities
- BRAC, simulation, and Army visions

Figure 31

Even if large parcels cannot offset home station land requirements, the land initiatives presented in Figure 7 are a scattered list with little correspondence to the Army's most critical land needs. Critical land-constrained posts like Forts Stewart or Lewis do not have land initiatives, while far less important and less constrained posts, like Orchard, are involved in seeking new lands. This has led to land-grab charges. The lack of a priority system for land initiatives was mentioned in each of the critical studies discussed in Figure 21.

As indicated in Figure 31, the next section of the briefing will deal with the issue of setting priorities for land initiatives.

When To Seek Expansion?

	Vacant federal land nearby?	Military importance?	Local support?
NTC	Yes	Very high	No
Mountain Home	Some	High	No
Bragg	No	Moderate	Yes

Figure 32

Is it possible to establish a list of initiatives based on military needs and implement such a list? Figure 32 highlights three characteristics of what were perhaps the three most significant military land initiatives of the last 15 years. Although the Mountain Home, Idaho initiative was conducted by the Air Force, the political lessons are similar for all the services.

In terms of military requirements and the availability of land, the NTC expansion would appear to have been both the most important and the most feasible. There is no more critical Army installation than the NTC, and it is surrounded by vacant federal land managed by the Bureau of Land Management. The Fort Bragg expansion was intended to create additional habitat for the RCW and had only indirect military benefits. Fort Bragg is located in a region of greater population density than the other two initiatives, and there is little nearby federal land. The expansion at Mountain Home, Idaho

(Figure 8) occurred in a somewhat less desolate area than the NTC expansion and was a critical military priority for the Air Force.

The only advantage of the Fort Bragg initiative was local and state political support. NTC and Idaho had at best only mixed levels of local support, and there was significant opposition.

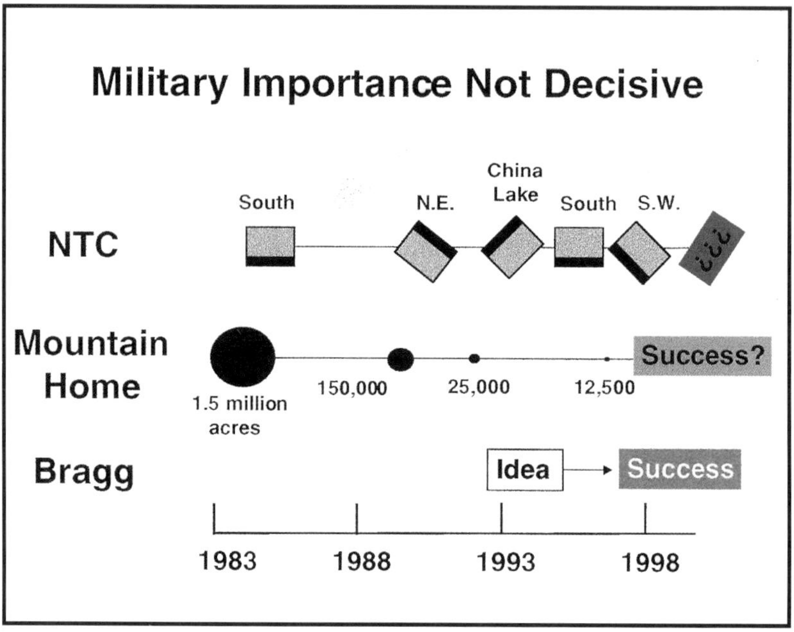

Figure 33

Figure 33 shows the history of the three initiatives described in Figure 32. These histories demonstrate that local political support, not military significance, is the most important variable in determining the outcome of an initiative.

THE NATIONAL TRAINING CENTER

The U.S. Army has been formally planning to expand Fort Irwin's National Training Center since 1985 and informally planning for an even longer period. The NTC is used to conduct force-on-force training exercises. An elaborate instrumentation system allows for actual simulated combat and the opportunity for combat units to replay their experiences.

Fort Irwin currently comprises 643,000 acres, with approximately 331,000 acres available for maneuver training.[32] The installation is large enough to operate brigade (–) force-on-force battles consisting of two battalions and brigade-level support. Many Army planners have wanted to expand Fort Irwin to allow for full brigade battles.

The evolution of the NTC expansion proposal is so complex that it seems impossible that anyone could have foreseen the outcome or the controversy when the initiative was launched. Specifically, the nearly 15-year-old initiative has been buffeted by four major factors:

- The biology of the desert tortoise and the emergence of a respiratory disease that ultimately led to the species being listed under the Endangered Species Act.
- Disagreement among local offices of federal land management agencies and the extension of that conflict to Washington and the legislative battles related to the California Desert Protection Act (CDPA).
- The emergence of a coalition of ranchers, hunters, off-road enthusiasts, and environmentalists opposed to Army land expansion.
- The unique pattern of private land ownership in the potential expansion areas and other areas affected by the CDPA.

The first formal output of the initiative was the first LURS study, which was completed in 1985 and documented a training shortfall of 238,000 acres. That same year, the Training Center Land Acquisition Project began, with the goal of expanding toward the south.[33] In

---

[32]Fort Irwin LURS study, submitted to Forces Command 20 September 1993. The LURS reports a deficit in being able to accommodate large training events and in the total of all events as described in Figure 7. The LURS reported that the armored cavalry squadron advance guard mission opposed by a motorized rifle regiment forward would require 611,573 acres and that the armored cavalry regiment rotation would require 732,513 acres. In addition, the 300,000 available maneuver acres is divided into roughly three separate smaller areas due to terrain constraints. See pages 13–14 of the LURS.

[33]An excellent history of the early years of the expansion effort can be found in Anne Chapman, *The National Training Center Matures: 1985–1993*, TRADOC Historical Monograph Series, Military History Office, U.S. Army Training and Doctrine Command, 1997.

1987 the Army Chief of Staff approved the effort, and in 1989 the Department of Defense filed the formal application with the Bureau of Land Management to "withdraw" additional public lands and began the Environmental Impact Statement project. At the same time, concern about an upper respiratory tract infection in the desert tortoise led the U.S. Fish and Wildlife Service to use its emergency powers to formally list the tortoise as a threatened species under the Endangered Species Act.[34] The listing meant that a formal consultation with the Fish and Wildlife Service would be required before a withdrawal could occur.

Since Army expansion plans were toward the south, which contained prime tortoise habitat, the proposal was delayed to allow studies of the potential impact on the tortoise. Although off-road vehicles, utility conduits, disease, and predators (the predatory raven population grew along with urban development in the Mojave Desert) all contributed to the demise of the tortoise population, the Fish and Wildlife Service concluded that the expansion was not consistent with the continued viability of the species. A draft jeopardy biological opinion was circulated and the Army abandoned its plans to expand to the south.[35]

From 1993 to 1997, the Army's central objective was to expand the NTC to the east and northeast. This alternative was less desirable because geological boundaries meant that additional maneuver area would not be created. However, the new lands could be used to station logistical support units currently occupying maneuver land on the NTC. Debate in Congress over the California Desert Protection Act (CDPA) slowed the proposal, as some versions of the legislation designated protected wilderness areas within the expansion areas. The local Bureau of Land Management consistently argued that Fort Irwin should attempt to share land with the China Lake Naval Weapons Laboratory directly to the northwest of the NTC. China

---

[34]The normal process for listing a species requires formal scientific studies and can take 18 months or more. The Fish and Wildlife Service has the authority to list a species on an emergency basis if the delay is thought to be a critical factor in its survivability.

[35]The Fish and Wildlife Service issues a jeopardy biological opinion when it determines that a federal action is likely to jeopardize the continued existence of listed species or result in the destruction or adverse modification of critical habitat.

Lake undertook a compatibility study in the mid-1990s and concluded that the presence of sensitive equipment, air pollution concerns, and scheduling problems would preclude joint use of this land.

The Army released a draft EIS in 1996 that contained alternatives for expansion in several directions. The EIS was released for public review in January 1997. With the final version of the 1993 CDPA not including wilderness areas in the expansion area, the Army seemed prepared to push for the northeast expansion. However, a new opportunity created by the CDPA opened up the possibility of once again redirecting the expansion to the south or the southwest. The CDPA established new national parks, preserves, and wilderness areas. It also required that the Bureau of Land Management and the National Park Service buy out private land holders still retaining parcels in these protected areas. However, neither agency had the funds to make these acquisitions, and the CDPA is not yet fully implemented.

Early in 1998 an idea emerged that reopened the southern expansion alternative. Army funds could be used to purchase private lands both inside and outside the expansion areas, with lands purchased outside the expansion area serving as mitigation for the damage to the desert tortoise that might occur due to the expansion.

Currently the details of a potential arrangement are still being negotiated among the Army, the land management agencies, the private land holders, and key members of Congress. An outline of alternative versions of this plan was presented at RAND by the Fort Irwin expansion project, placing the cost of the mitigation between $44 and $81 million depending on whether the southwest or southern expansion was approved. Total costs included other land purchases, improvements, and relocation costs, moving the total expansion cost up to $113 million and $177 million, depending on whether a southwest or southern expansion was being proposed.

In examining the merits of the alternative proposals for a southward or southwestern expansion, the Army should recall that the proposal is both expensive and is similar to an earlier proposal that led to a jeopardy biological opinion. The Army should be prepared to answer the following questions before proceeding:

1. Are the new mitigation techniques biologically effective so that the expansion will not be vulnerable to a lawsuit, or are they a product of a short-sighted political desire to implement CDPA?
2. Will the legislation withdrawing the land protect the Army from potential lawsuits by establishing the mitigation as being adequate?
3. Is money for the expansion being added to the Army budget, or must the Army choose between the expansion and other funding priorities?
4. Will the expansion be adequate if Army training land requirements increase drastically, such as might occur in some Army After Next concepts? Or will it be necessary to utilize the entire Fort Irwin/China Lake complex to meet these needs? If so, does the southward or southwest expansion facilitate access to China Lake?
5. Given the political, biological, and financial risks associated with a southward expansion, is the northeast preferable?

However this initiative unfolds, it seems clear that the outcome is still not predictable. It was certainly not predictable 15 years ago when the project was initiated.

AIR FORCE OPERATIONS IN IDAHO

As illustrated by the advertisement in Figure 8, Air Force efforts to acquire additional land in Idaho were at least as contentious as efforts to expand the NTC. They have taken an equally long time and have followed an equally unpredictable path.

The earliest discussions of expanding Air Force operations in Idaho date back to the early 1980s, when the Air Force contemplated the acquisition of several million acres in southeastern Idaho. One source claims that the initial interest was motivated by close personal connections between senior Air Force officials and leading Idaho politicians anxious to keep Mountain Home Air Force base off future base closure lists. The first formal proposal, presented in 1987, was a plan to expand the existing Saylor Creek bombing range by 1.5 million acres.

From the start, the proposal clashed with a coalition of environmentalists, ranchers, Native Americans, and other users of the public land. These constituencies coalesced to oppose Air Force initiatives and made important connections to the White House and other decisionmakers in Washington. The proposal also became tangled with the aircraft-restationing efforts that provided the military justification for the land. The Air Force seemed to justify the restationing on the basis of the new range while justifying the new range on the basis of the restationing. At the same time, the Air Force separated the Environmental Impact Statements for the restationing and expansion. The process exacerbated the Air Force's relationship with the public and was ultimately held in violation of the NEPA.

During the almost 15 years of effort, the Air Force proposal has gone through four distinct stages. The first involved the 1.5-million-acre proposal known as the Saylor Creek Range expansion. By 1990 the 150,000 Big Springs proposal had replaced Saylor Creek. The Air Force then downsized the effort to a 25,000-acre expansion known as the Idaho Training Range (ITR). This proposal was abandoned because a court ruled that separate studies for restationing and land expansion violated NEPA, and also because of the influence of key members of the local coalition with the White House.

Since 1994 the Air Force has been working to develop a smaller 12,500-acre expansion known as Enhanced Training in Idaho (ETI). The Air Force has gone through extensive efforts to develop mitigation measures and work with the local constituents. The Air Force recently filed a Record of Decision (ROD), and Congress approved the withdrawal in the FY99 budget bill. However, the Air Force has not started construction of the range facilities, or started using the range, due to pending lawsuits.

Although the Air Force may have finally succeeded, the initiative speaks to the unpredictability of land initiatives and the political costs that an entire military service may incur from a single land initiative. No one would have imagined the difficulty and compromises needed to acquire the current 12,000 acres. Some argue that the mitigation efforts, particularly related to new restrictions on airspace use, make the expansion of little military value. As indicated by the question mark in the success box in Figure 33, it is difficult to label the overall initiative as a success story.

FORT BRAGG

In 1992, RAND performed a study on the impact of environmental restrictions on military training at Fort Bragg.[36] A series of recommendations were made, including the possibility of acquiring additional land. At the time, base personnel informed us that some available land did exist outside the base boundaries. However, they were concerned that much of it was fragmented and that it would be politically difficult to acquire.

Supported by the sudden availability of a large parcel housing a former estate and the active involvement of its senators, who ensured that funds for a land acquisition would be available, Fort Bragg was able to quickly acquire an additional 10,000 acres. As discussed in Figures 22a and 22b, there are numerous military and ecological reasons for seeking additional land at Fort Bragg. Indeed, the primary motivation was to increase the size of the Fort Bragg RCW habitat so that population goals could be more easily obtained and restrictions on training eventually relaxed. Additional NEPA documentation would be required if Fort Bragg chose to use this 10,000 acres for training.

Whereas both Idaho and the NTC expansions were directed toward areas with minimal population, the area around Fort Bragg consists of varied terrain with some small towns, farms, and forests. Nevertheless, land became available and there was strong political support for the initiative.

---

[36]David Rubenson, Jerome Aroesty, and Charles Thompsen, *Two Shades of Green: Environmental Protection and Combat Training*, Santa Monica, CA: RAND, R-4220-A, 1992.

Political Issues Overwhelm Military Needs

- **Most "home stations" benefit from expansion**
- **Limited land available**
- **Basis for proceeding:**
  - Available land
  - Local political support
- **Military significance has little impact**

"Targets of opportunity" the only approach

Figure 34

The previously cited reports criticized the Army for the lack of a national land strategy, the failure to consider Army-wide lands when assessing individual installation needs, and for an implementation strategy based on "targets of opportunity." But these studies failed to consider the politics of land expansion. The constraints imposed by political concerns, in combination with the assessment in Figures 23 and 26—that all home stations would benefit from additional land (even if not essential)—force the Army into a "target of opportunity" approach to land initiatives. Any effort to develop a more "rational" national priority system based on military needs would fail.

The rational approach fails because DoD does not have an opportunity to design a set of alternatives aimed at providing maximum military utility. The competition for land, both public and private, is so intense that there are few opportunities for land initiatives in general. Those that do emerge, such as the availability of the Rockefeller Estate outside Fort Bragg or the California BLM's very recent efforts to redirect the Fort Irwin initiative to the south, emerge from local considerations that may have little to do with DoD. Efforts of the DoD to design initiatives, such as the original NTC proposal or Mountain Home, will at best be severely modified by the political process and can place the military in the middle of a political firestorm with significant organizational and political costs. There is no opportunity to identify a systematic set of land initiatives that will satisfy training needs. Pursuing such initiatives will lead to numerous failures and the expenditure of significant organizational energy.

A more realistic approach would first acknowledge that virtually every Forces Command home station would benefit from additional land, even if it is not absolutely essential. It would also recognize that there are few opportunities to expand these home stations because of the lack of available land. If land becomes available, and the local community supports the military acquiring or using that land, then the chance of success would move this "target of opportunity" to the top of any rational national priority system. The broad-based need for land, coupled with the geographical isolation of individual bases, makes it difficult to argue that such an opportunity should be discarded because a different initiative is being pursued elsewhere. Headquarters already evaluates individual initiatives for financial and political implications, and there seems to be no reason to force a comparison of different initiatives.

In summary, the inability to design attractive land initiatives with predictable outcome and costs, as well as the physical and political fragmentation of individual installations, preclude the development of a rational nationwide priority system for land initiatives. Instead, a strategy that recognizes that many Army installations would benefit from additional land, and pursues such goals when the local community supports them, is consistent with both military needs and the constraints of land politics. A "target of opportunity" strategy reflects community wishes and military needs. It is not the same as an unnecessary acquisition.

Chapter Five

BRAC, SIMULATION, AND ARMY VISIONS

Outline

- Top-down: importance of a national strategy
- The DoD (Army) land base
  - Organizational boundaries
  - Physical boundaries
- Bottom-up
  - Installation needs/Army resources
  - Setting priorities
- → BRAC, simulation, and Army visions

Figure 35

In this section we will discuss how changes in simulation technology and opportunities for additional rounds of the Base Realignment and Closure Process (BRAC) could alter the preceding discussion.

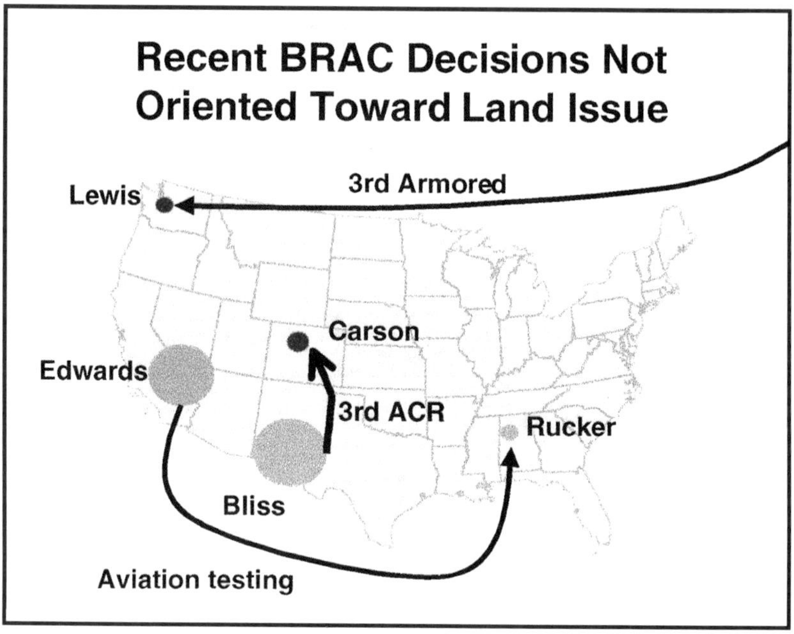

Figure 36

There have been four previous BRAC rounds. Many of the actions involved the closure of "postage stamp" installations in an effort to reduce aggregate base operating costs.

Figure 36 illustrates several realignment actions that suggest land use considerations were not a major factor in decisionmaking. The examples may even suggest that organizational boundaries acted to prevent the use of BRAC as a tool for rationalizing military land use.

Figure 36 shows the 3rd Armored Cavalry Regiment moving from Fort Bliss to Fort Carson. The ACR is one of the most maneuverable units in the Army, and the vast expanse of Fort Bliss offered significant training advantages. Fort Carson is small, and large maneuvers require deployment to the Piñon Canyon Training Center 150 miles away. Different Army sources have cited alternative reasons for this transfer. One possibility may have been the desire to station the ACR on a Forces Command base (Fort Carson) rather than on a TRADOC base (Fort Bliss).

The decision to realign the 3rd Armored Division from Europe to Fort Lewis also had little basis in attempting to rationalize land use. The Environmental Impact Statement listed Fort Bliss as the primary alternative and argued that Bliss had superior training lands. But Bliss lacked adequate facilities, and the decision was made to move the division to Fort Lewis.

Finally, the decision to move the Army's aviation testing units from Edwards Air Force Base to Fort Rucker suggests a lack of consideration for airspace. Edwards sits under one of the largest blocks of restricted military airspace in the country and is the site of declining levels of activity. Fort Rucker's airspace is confined to a nine-mile box.

Figures 15, 16a, and 16b portrayed a mismatch between the locations of the Army's units and lands. Previous BRAC rounds were not used to end this mismatch, and organizational boundaries may have acted to exacerbate it.

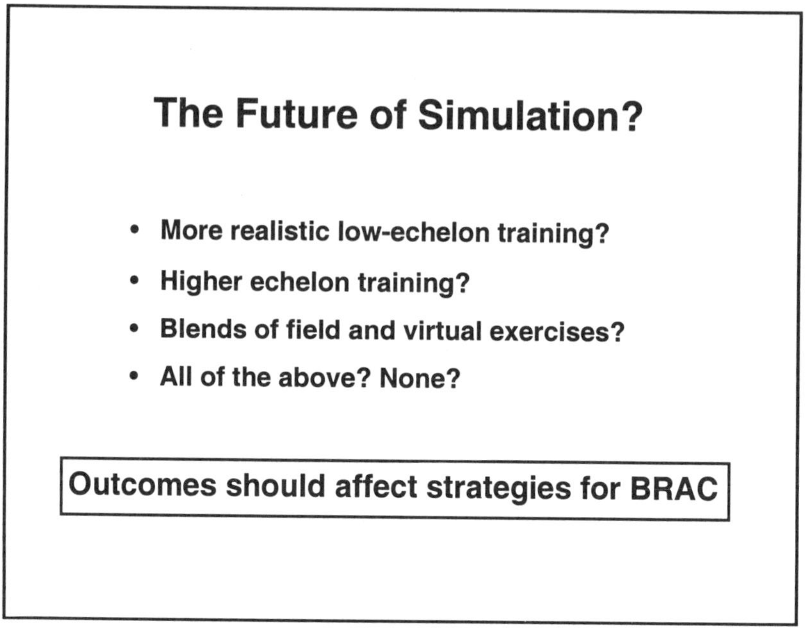

Figure 37

Figure 37 suggests several potential outcomes of Army simulation work and suggests that the way in which simulation progresses should be part of the decisionmaking in determining which bases to close in a future BRAC.

The current status of simulation technology was summarized in Figure 24. However, the current status is only a reference point for a research program that began a decade ago and will continue. According to the Army Modeling and Simulation (M&S) Investment Plan, the Army will spend $2.3 billion on modeling and simulation in the next five years, mostly in the Training, Exercises, and Military Operations (TEMO) domain.

The Army is committed to improving the realism of small-unit simulation training and to developing simulations at all echelons. Obviously there is significant uncertainty as to which developments will be most successful. One possibility is that, in the long run, an increasing fraction of small-unit training could be done with simulations, freeing up funds to visit large ranges for the larger maneuvers.[37] We may also see an increased ability to blend activities from different installations, thus providing greater connectivity among fragmented Army parcels. Units operating virtual equipment may be able to interact with units conducting field exercises at a different installation.

CCTT

In the coming years, we can expect continued improvement in the CCTT (described below Figure 24) to possibly allow the Army to conduct much of its small-unit training in the simulated world. Currently, CCTT is used for no larger than company-level training, though battalion-level training would not require any major breakthroughs to achieve. Fort Hood has a sufficient number of machines and sufficient terrain data to lay the basis for modifications that would allow battalion-level training.

The Army M&S Investment Plan states that unit readiness will be enhanced due to the seamless connectivity of units *at all echelons* (emphasis added) to exercise with realistic representations of friendly and enemy capabilities. It is possible that the CCTT will be stretched to fill the gap, although near-term improvements may focus on improving the quality of platoon and company operations (e.g., capturing higher-resolution terrain, improving the modeling of semi-automated forces, and other measures rather than enlarging the battlespace).

IMPROVED COMMAND AND STAFF EXERCISES

Programs like the Battle Command Training Program (BCTP) and Warfighters Simulation (WARSIM) 2000 as part of the Joint Simulation System (JSIMS) will provide warfighting exercises for command and staff. These programs are conceived as part of a joint vision

---

[37]We note that under today's budget constraints there is no reduction of field training when CCTT is available. Field training budgets are so low that simulation is viewed as a supplement to field training, not as even a partial substitute.

shared by the services, so they are intended to be interoperable with Navy and Air Force systems.

BLENDING OF LIVE AND SIMULATED ENTITIES IN TRAINING EVENTS

The technical framework for seamlessly blending live and simulated units has been laid. The DMSO-sponsored High Level Architecture (HLA), the Army's Synthetic Theater of War-Architecture (STOW-A), and the Joint Technical Architecture (JTA) will foster integration of live and simulated units across installations, commands, and services.[38] However, these technical architectures are only the beginning step in a long design and development process to achieve the desired interoperable simulations of the future. Current efforts to blend activities at different locations known as the Advanced Warfighting Experiments (AWE) are slow and only useful in an experimental format.

UNCERTAINTY IN FUTURE PROSPECTS FOR TRAINING SIMULATION

While the DoD-wide technical architectures and advances in computing infrastructure lay a solid foundation for training simulation, the challenge will be to take the technology from testbeds to mainstream unit training. Furthermore, there is a strong desire to have the systems that the Army uses be the same as the systems used for mission rehearsal and actual combat. To achieve these objectives, the Army commands and the acquisition and training communities will need to work more closely to integrate their modeling and simulation efforts. Most crucial is the adoption of the new technology across the spectrum of planning, training, and active/reserve communities.

The different operating environments, cultures, and doctrine of the various military services present significant hurdles in the development of truly interoperable training simulations. These hurdles in-

---

[38]DMSO is the Defense Modeling and Simluation Office.

troduce additional uncertainty about the ultimate effectiveness and scope of modeling and simulation for training.

Whatever the outcome, these technology developments may have important effects on land requirements. But even if they do not, some outside the military may still assume that they do.[39] Currently, cost savings are the primary motivation for simulation research. Although the Training Directorate in DSCOPS and TRADOC's Army Training and Support Center consider the effect of simulation on land needs, the idea of a tradeoff has not penetrated a broader Army constituency.

---

[39]A recent study by the DoD Inspector General suggested that there is still insufficient data to determine the effectiveness of the simulation technology that has been developed to date. Audit Report 97-138, April 30, 1997.

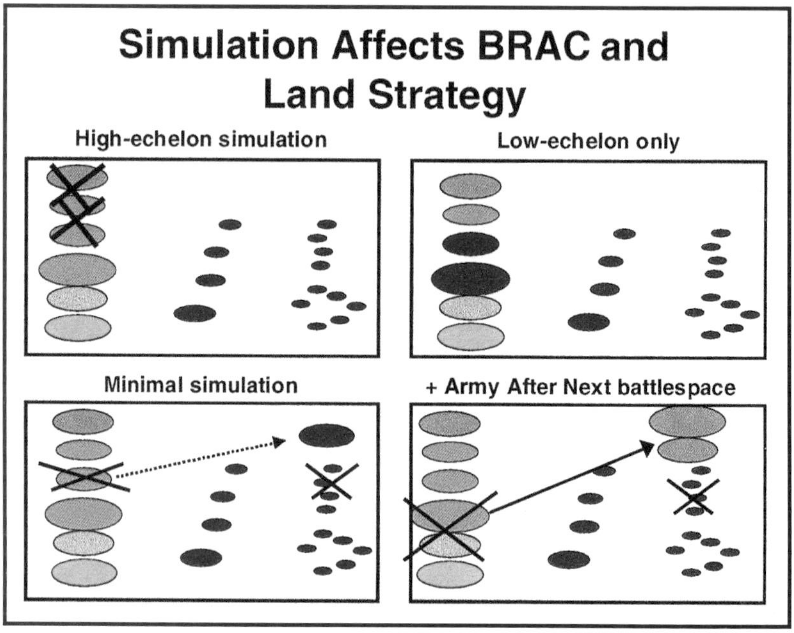

Figure 38

Figure 38 uses an abbreviated form of the schematic displayed in Figure 14 to illustrate the relationship among BRAC, simulation technology, and land use.

Each of the four diagrams shows "large ranges," "training centers," and the Forces Command "home stations." The "postage stamps" are not illustrated in the diagrams. The diagram in the upper left shows the implications if simulation technology is successful in achieving realistic higher-echelon training. If this occurs, the underutilized "large ranges" may be less valuable as a strategic land reserve, and it may be desirable to close one or more facilities if there is insufficient test activity to justify their continued operation. In this situation, training requirements would have little impact on the need to preserve these large parcels, and a decision to close such a parcel would be based entirely on test requirements.

In the upper right diagram we assume that simulation technology is effective at providing realistic lower-echelon training but not at higher echelons. In this case substantial savings might be realized by conducting most low-echelon training in the simulator. This would free up funds to allow units to access large ranges for temporary training. We have colored two of the large ranges blue to indicate that in such a circumstance, either the ranges should be transferred to Forces Command or the organizational obstacles discussed in Figure 28 must be overcome.

The diagram in the lower left portrays the situation where simulation has little impact on training requirements. If the trend in battlespace growth continues, the Army may want to contemplate converting Fort Bliss or a large test range into a home station. The arrow pointing from "large ranges" to the "home stations" indicates this transfer. The Army would need a long-term plan to finance and build the necessary infrastructure on the relevant "large ranges."

If some of the more ambitious and dispersed Army After Next concepts are realized, it is difficult to imagine how the Army will find locations to accomplish realistic field training. One possibility is the contiguous Fort Bliss and White Sands land area. Another is represented by the four large bases, one from each service, in the Mojave Desert (Fort Irwin, China Lake, Edwards AFB, and 29 Palms Marine Base). Although they are not all contiguous, they are close enough and provide enough land to envision use of the air mobility discussed in Army After Next. This is represented by the transfer of several "large ranges" to DoD (purple) "home stations" in the lower right diagram.

Chapter Six

CONCLUSIONS

Conclusions

- **Physical boundaries make "aggregate needs and lands" meaningless**
- **Most "home stations" constrained and isolated**
- **Army has coherent, but implicit, strategy**
  - **Organizational boundaries inhibit explanation**
  - **Difficult to "prioritize" initiatives**
- **Organizational boundaries could inhibit BRAC and simulation in land strategy**
  - **Large ranges important**
  - **Comprehensive basing study needed**

Figure 39

Figure 39 presents the general conclusions of the briefing. We find that the physical distance between Army installations effectively isolates them. While internal organizational boundaries do exist and could inhibit efficient use of the total resource, these obstacles are small compared to the costs of moving units among installations. Concepts such as "Army-wide" lands or the ability to sacrifice land expansions in some areas, if they proceed elsewhere, are meaningless.

The active Army's "home stations" are small and isolated. Each would benefit from additional land. However, the Army uses a diverse set of techniques involving simulation, visits to "training centers," and training tools to offset land shortfalls. *In answer to the question posed in the title of this briefing, we conclude that the Army does have a coherent land strategy.* Unfortunately, it is an implicit one. It is also a strategy within the confines of political obstacles to major realignments. The Army does not have a strategy in place should there be opportunities to achieve a major realignment of units.

The Army's formal methodology for calculating land requirements ignores this strategy, both because it is an implicit one and because of the organizational boundaries within each level of command. Those implementing TC 25-1 are not the combat units that have improvised to cope with land shortages. The result is that Army needs can become exaggerated and that the implicit acquisition strategy is left unexplained, undermining the credibility of land initiatives. We also find that the call for the Army to rationalize land initiatives by military importance is not realistic. A wide range of Army bases would benefit from additional land, but it is local political support and the availability of land—not military significance—that determine whether any land can be acquired. Military significance is a prerequisite for gaining any political support, but it does not determine the ultimate outcome.

The politics of land use imply that it will be increasingly difficult for the Army to satisfy its demands for training land through expansion. Simulation technology development and realignment are two alternative ways of attacking the problem. However, these alternatives have not made a strong impression across the Army. The Army must overcome internal organizational boundaries that inhibit the integration of land issues into these two processes.

Proper integration of these factors will lead to increased attention to the future of the "large ranges." These ranges constitute the Army's training land reserve but are not recognized as such by the current major command structure. The Army needs to conduct a comprehensive basing study that considers all Army assets without regard to internal organizational boundaries.

Programmatic Recommendations

- Make implicit strategy explicit
- Host training conference on TC 25-1
- Reexamine two cases:
  - NTC/China Lake
  - Bliss/White Sands
- Work test-training range institutional issues
  - Bliss/White Sands site for case study
- Track simulation for land impacts
- Conduct strategic basing study
  - Cross command
  - Cross service
- Work toward Bliss renewal in 99-606 process
- Analyze converting "large range" to home station

Figure 40

Figure 40 highlights the programmatic conclusions that emerge from the briefing.

The physical isolation of Army installations implies that a national land strategy (under the assumption that there are no opportunities for significant realignments) will produce little substantive change in policy. Nevertheless, the absence of such a strategy has been a confusing point that has damaged Army and military land initiatives. TC 25-1, which misses key aspects of the Army's implicit strategy, worsens the situation. We therefore recommend that the Army publish a land strategy for the purpose of explaining its current actions and policies. To do this, the Army should convene an internal conference composed of land managers and trainers to resolve problems in TC 25-1.

We reached the general conclusion that physical, not organizational, boundaries are the major factor inhibiting efficient use of the Army's total resource. However, Fort Irwin/China Lake and Bliss/White Sands are possible exceptions. The Army should reexamine these cases and answer the questions regarding the Fort Irwin expansion highlighted in Figure 33.

Although physical boundaries were more significant, organizational boundaries, particularly those acting to discourage the use of test ranges by training units, are not insignificant. The Army should identify the obstacles and organize a plan to overcome them. Given the declining activity at White Sands and the need for additional space for Fort Bliss's Roving Sands exercise, this may constitute an ideal opportunity for an experiment aimed at overcoming these obstacles.

The Army should reemphasize its effort to consider the implications of simulation technology on land use. At present the Integrated Training Area Management Program in ODSCOPS and the Army Training and Support Center at TRADOC have responsibility for considering this linkage. Both institutions have been emphasizing the implications of environmental issues on training land. It would be consistent with their charters and require only a slight shift in emphasis for these offices to conduct a thorough examination of this issue.

As noted in the previous chart, the Army (or DoD) should prepare for future BRACs by conducting an Army-wide (DoD-wide) basing study that is not bound by the existing organizational boundaries within the Department of Defense.

The 600,000-acre McGregor Range at Fort Bliss is subject to the renewal process as stipulated under Public Law 99-606. The Fort Bliss/White Sands complex may be the only location where the Army can conduct field training for some of the Army After Next concepts. Fort Bliss is the only "large range" in the lower 48 states that is part of the Army's training base. The Army should therefore actively seek the renewal of McGregor Range as an important hedge against future requirements.

Finally, we recommend that the Army conduct a conceptual study on the steps needed to convert a "large range" to a home station. Such a conversion could represent a significant step in overcoming land shortages, but the costs and obstacles are significant. The Army should examine alternatives and consider phased strategies that would allow greater use of its land reserves.

We conclude by answering the five policy questions listed below Figure 2.

- **Why is it important to have a coherent national military land strategy?**

The military has a long-term need to access land for military training and testing. There is intense competition for land, and land-use decisions are made in political forums not directly concerned with military affairs. The military can best defend its needs by developing a coherent strategy that can be understood by policymakers outside the Department of Defense. Such a strategy must explain why there could be an aggregate oversupply along with local shortages.

- **What organizational boundaries divide DoD land resources? What physical boundaries?**

The military land base is divided into by military services, the major commands within each service, subcommands, and individual installations. At each level there are intraorganizational boundaries between land managers and land users. With some exceptions, the Army's land base is physically divided into small-isolated-overcrowded installations in the East (mostly) and large open ranges in the West.

- **How does the Army determine land needs, and how would a strategy that minimizes the role of organizational boundaries change decisionmaking?**

The Army compares local land needs with local resources. It does not consider "Army-wide" lands. The methodology suffers from the intra-agency organizational boundaries by failing to account for the implicit strategy used to cope with land shortages. An approach that overcomes this obstacle would give a more realistic and understandable assessment of Army needs. But it would not change decisionmaking, because it is the physical boundaries that prevent optimized use of the total military land resource.

- **How much land does the Army need?**

In the absence of an opportunity to realign units and bases, the physical boundaries in the Army land base make the issue of total Army needs meaningless. Each installation's resources, and the tools that can be used to offset land shortages, must be evaluated individually.

- **How will these answers change with new developments in simulation technology or with additional rounds of BRAC?**

One means of addressing the physical boundaries is to realign military units to better match land resources. Developments in simulation technology could change the type of BRAC actions that would be needed. However, there is little organizational attention given to the land use implications of BRAC or simulation technology. Some past BRAC actions have even worked against a rationalization of military land usage.

Appendix A

MAJOR ARMY LAND HOLDINGS

Army Facility	Military Personnel	Acres	Personnel/ Acre	Command
Fort Myer, VA	2,900	256	11.3281	WMD
Fort McNair, Washington, DC	650	89	7.3034	WMD
Presidio of Monterey, CA	2,500	395	6.3291	FC
Fort McPherson, GA	2,500	487	5.1335	FC
Tripler Army Medical Center, HI	1,761	360	4.8917	AMC
Fort Sam Houston, TX	12,000	3,160	3.7975	FC
Fort Hamilton, NY	465	152	3.0592	USAR
Charles Melvin Price Support Center, IL	1,500	686	2.1866	AMC
Fort Meade, MD	9,000	5,415	1.6620	WMD
Carlisle Barracks, PA	723	440	1.6432	TRA
Fort Monroe, VA	849	568	1.4947	WMD
Fort Story, VA	2,070	1,451	1.4266	WMD
Fort Shafter, HI	1,400	1,400	1.0000	PAC
Walter Reed Army Medical Center	10	10	1.0000	AMC
U.S. Army Garrison, Fitzsimmons, CO	550	576	0.9549	USAR
Fort Ritchie, MD	608	638	0.9530	WMD
Schofield Barracks, HI	12,156	14,000	0.8683	PAC
Hunter Army Airfield, GA	4,226	5,370	0.7870	FC
Fort Detrick, MD	935	1,200	0.7792	WMD
Fort Eustis, VA	5,484	8,239	0.6656	AMC
Fort Monmouth, NJ	824	1,344	0.6131	AMC
Fort Leavenworth, KS	3,200	5,600	0.5714	TRA
Fort Lee, VA	3,016	5,575	0.5410	WMD
Detroit Arsenal, MI	170	341	0.4985	AMC
Fort Belvoir, VA	4,300	8,656	0.4968	AMC
Fort Gillem, GA	660	1,394	0.4735	AMC
West Point, NY	4,983	16,000	0.3114	TRA

Army Facility	Military Personnel	Acres	Personnel/ Acre	Command
Fort Bragg, NC	43,000	148,618	0.2893	FC
Rock Island Arsenal, IL	260	946	0.2748	AMC
Fort Jackson, SC	12,679	52,301	0.2424	TRA
Fort Lewis, WA	20,000	86,176	0.2321	FC
Fort Campbell, KY	23,299	105,068	0.2218	FC
Military Ocean Terminal, Bayonne, NJ	94	437	0.2151	AMC
Fort Gordon, GA	11,305	55,588	0.2034	TRA
Fort Hood, TX	41,000	217,337	0.1886	FC
Fort Sill, OK	16,490	94,220	0.1750	TRA
Fort Leonard Wood, MO	10,880	63,000	0.1727	TRA
Fort Benning, GA	21,119	182,000	0.1160	TRA
Fort Riley, KS	10,599	100,000	0.1060	FC
Fort Carson, CO	14,302	137,000	0.1044	FC
Fort McClellan, AL	4,761	46,000	0.1035	TRA
Fort Knox, KY	11,000	109,000	0.1009	TRA
Fort Drum, NY	10,500	107,265	0.0979	FC
Cold Regions Research Laboratory	3	31	0.0968	ACE
Oakland Army Base, CA	37	422	0.0877	AMC
Fort Huachuca, AZ	5,670	73,272	0.0774	TRA
Fort Rucker, AL	4,793	63,232	0.0758	TRA
Construction Engineering Research Laboratory	2	33	0.0606	ACE
Aberdeen Proving Grounds, MD	4,233	72,500	0.0584	TRA
Fort Stewart, GA	15,917	279,000	0.0571	FC
Tobyhanna Army Depot, PA	50	1,300	0.0385	AMC
Fort Polk, LA	7,432	198,000	0.0375	FC
Corpus Christi Army Depot, TX	5	150	0.0333	AMC
Fort Richardson, AK	2,113	73,100	0.0289	PAC
Waterways Experiment Station, MS	15	673	0.0223	ACE
Watervliet Arsenal, NY	3	140	0.0214	AMC
Picatinny Arsenal, NJ	117	6,400	0.0183	AMC
Fort Bliss, TX	12,000	1,200,000	0.0100	TRA
Fort Irwin, CA	4,694	642,000	0.0073	FC
Redstone Arsenal, AL	474	67,000	0.0071	AMC
Fort Dix, NJ	200	31,000	0.0065	FC
Pine Bluff Arsenal, AR	81	14,500	0.0056	AMC
Fort Wainwright, AK	4,600	916,000	0.0050	PAC
Sierra Army Depot, CA	50	36,000	0.0014	AMC

Army Facility	Military Personnel	Acres	Personnel/ Acre	Command
Fort A.P. Hill, VA	83	76,000	0.0011	WMD
Letterkenny Army Depot, PA	19	19,520	0.0010	AMC
Military Ocean Terminal, Sunny Point, NC	10	16,000	0.0006	AMC
Red River Army Depot, TX	10	19,900	0.0005	AMC
Fort Greely, AK	311	629,000	0.0005	PAC
Anniston Army Depot, AL	6	15,000	0.0004	AMC
Yakima Training Center, WA	125	323,400	0.0004	FC
Camp Bullis, TX	10	27,880	0.0004	FC
White Sands Missile Range, NM	707	2,000,000	0.0004	AMC
Yuma Proving Ground, AZ	350	1,000,000	0.0004	AMC
Tooele Army Depot, UT	8	23,000	0.0003	AMC
Umatilla Chemical Depot, OR	6	19,729	0.0003	AMC
Blue Grass Army Depot, KY	4	14,500	0.0003	AMC
Pohakuloa Training Area, APO AP, HI	22	108,792	0.0002	PAC
Seneca Army Depot Activity, NY	2	10,600	0.0002	AMC
Rocky Mountain Arsenal, CO	3	17,000	0.0002	AMC
Fort Indiantown Gap, PA	2	18,000	0.0001	USAR
Savanna Army Depot Activity, IL	1	13,000	0.0001	AMC
Dugway Proving Ground, UT	60	798,855	0.0001	AMC
Pueblo Chemical Depot, CO	1	23,000	0.0000	AMC
Piñon Canyon	10	236,000	0.0000	FC

Appendix B

TRAINING LAND REQUIREMENTS AND ACQUISITION MODEL (ATLAM)

(See the following page)

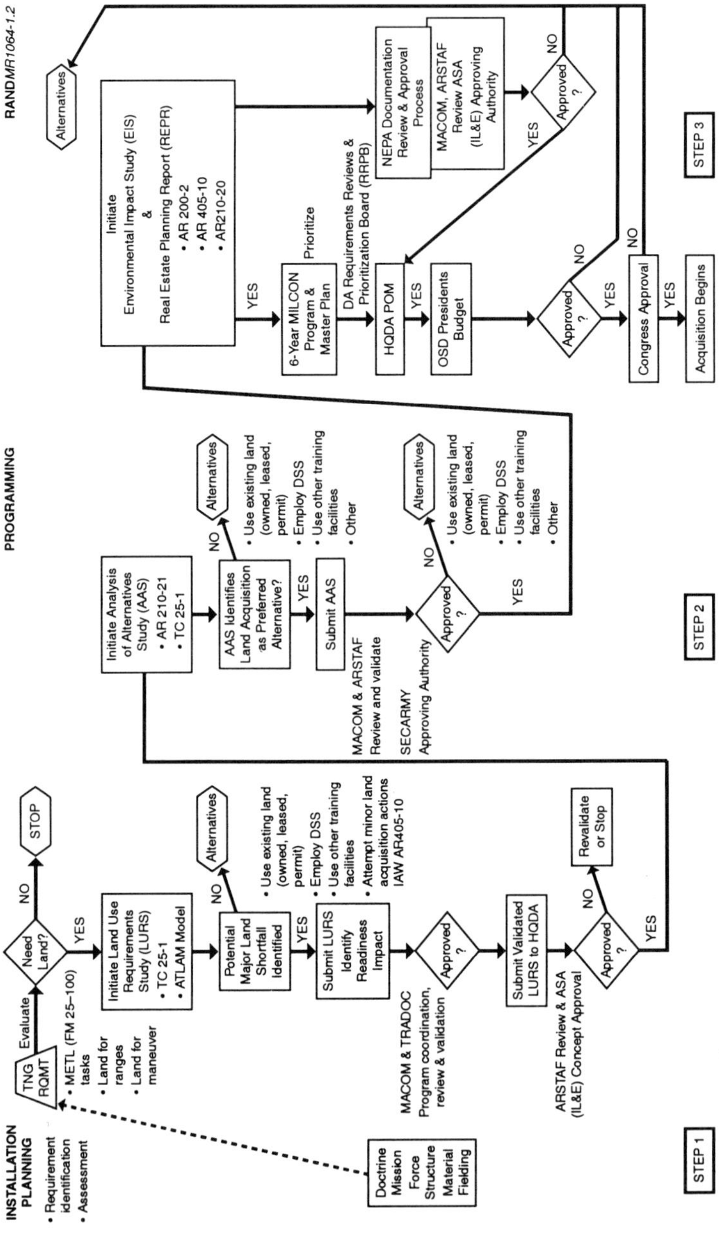

RANDMR1064-1.2
INSTALLATION PLANNING
• Requirement identification
• Assessment
PROGRAMMING
TNG RQMT
• METL (FM 25–100) tasks
• Land for ranges
• Land for maneuver
Evaluate
Need Land?
NO
STOP
YES
Initiate Land Use Requirements Study (LURS)
• TC 25-1
• ATLAM Model
Potential Major Land Shortfall Identified
NO
Alternatives
• Use existing land (owned, leased, permit)
• Employ DSS
• Use other training facilities
• Attempt minor land acquisition actions IAW AR405-10
YES
Submit LURS Identify Readiness Impact
Approved ?
MACOM & TRADOC Program coordination, review & validation
Submit Validated LURS to HQDA
Approved ?
ARSTAF Review & ASA (IL&E) Concept Approval
NO
Revalidate or Stop
YES
Doctrine Mission Force Structure Material Fielding
STEP 1
Initiate Analysis of Alternatives Study (AAS)
• AR 210-21
• TC 25-1
AAS Identifies Land Acquisition as Preferred Alternative?
NO
Alternatives
• Use existing land (owned, leased, permit)
• Employ DSS
• Use other training facilities
• Other
YES
Submit AAS
MACOM & ARSTAF Review and validate
SECARMY Approving Authority
Approved ?
NO
Alternatives
• Use existing land (owned, leased, permit)
• Employ DSS
• Use other training facilities
• Other
YES
STEP 2
Alternatives
Initiate Environmental Impact Study (EIS) & Real Estate Planning Report (REPR)
• AR 200-2
• AR 405-10
• AR210-20
YES
6-Year MILCON Program & Master Plan
Prioritize
DA Requirements Reviews & Prioritization Board (RRPB)
HQDA POM
YES
OSD Presidents Budget
Approved ?
NO
YES
Congress Approval
NO
YES
Acquisition Begins
NEPA Documentation Review & Approval Process
MACOM, ARSTAF Review ASA (IL&E) Approving Authority
Approved ?
NO
YES
STEP 3

Appendix C

HEAVY (MECHANIZED INFANTRY/ARMOR) DIVISION MANEUVER AREA REQUIREMENTS

Unit/Task	Density of Units	Land Requirements	Iterations to Maintain Proficiency	Days Required per Iteration	Gross Land Required per Task km^2 Days
Support Plt					
(ARTEP 17-236-11-MTP)	10				
Provide Log Spt	10	$20 \times 1 = 20$ km^2	3	1	600
Medical Plt					
(ARTEP 17-236-12-MTP)	10				
Provide Health Svc Spt	10	$8 \times 1 = 8$ km^2	3	1	240
Maintenance Plt					
(ARTEP 17-236-10-MTP)	10				
Provide Maint Spt	10	$3 \times 1.5 = 4.5$ km^2	3	1	135
Conduct Recovery Op	10	$3 \times 1.5 = 4.5$ km^2	3	1	135
Communications Plt					
(ARTEP 11-037-30-MTP)	10				
Provide Comm to TFCP	10	$1 \times 1 = 1$ km^2	3	1	30
Tank Company					
(ARTEP 71-1-MTP)	20				
Movement to Contact	20	$2.5 \times 12 = 30$ km^2	3	1	1,800
Offense	20	$2.25 \times 7 = 15.75$ km^2	3	1	945
Raid	20	$2.25 \times 7 = 15.75$ km^2	3	1	945
Defend	20	$2 \times 1.5 = 3$ km^2	3	1	1,800
Retrograde	20	$2.6 \times 9 = 24$ km^2	3	1	1,440
Recon & Security	20	$4 \times 4 = 16$ km^2	3	1	960

SOURCE: Army Training Circular 25-1.

Unit/Task	Density of Units	Land Requirements	Iterations to Maintain Proficiency	Days Required per Iteration	Gross Land Required per Task km^2 Days
Tank Platoon					
(ARTEP 17-237-10-MTP)	60				
Attack	60	$1 \times 3 = 3$ km^2	3	1	540
Defend	60	$.8 \times .4 = .32$ km^2	3	1	57.6
Armored Cav Sqdn					
(ARTEP 17-485-MTP)	1				
Recon Op	1	$20 \times 30 = 600$ km^2	2	1	1,200
Screening Op	1	$20 \times 30 = 600$ km^2	2	1	1,200

Appendix D

TRAINING ACTIVITY WITHIN MARKED BUFFER ZONES

Maneuver and Bivouac:	
Hasty defense, light infantry, hand digging only, 2 hours max	Yes
Hasty defense, mechanized infantry/armor 24 hours	No
Deliberate defense, light infantry 48 hours	No
Deliberate defense, mechanized infantry/armor	No
Establish command post, light infantry 36 hours	No
Establish command post, mechanized infantry/armor 36 hours	No
Assembly area operations, light infantry/mech infantry/armor	No
Establish CS/CSS sites	No
Establish signal sites	No
Foot transit through the colony	Yes
Wheeled vehicle transit through the colony (1)	Yes
Armored vehicle transit through the colony (1)	Yes
Cutting natural camouflage, hard wood only	Yes
Establish camouflage netting	No
Vehicle maintenance for no more than 2 hours	Yes
Weapons Firing:	
7.62 mm and below blank firing	Yes
.50 cal blank firing	Yes
Artillery firing point/position	No
MLRS firing position	No
All others	No

SOURCE: Fort Bragg Training and Mobilization Office.

Noise:	
Generators	No
Artillery/hand grenade simulators	Yes
Hoffman type devices	Yes
Pyrotechnics/Smoke:	
CS/riot agents	No
Smoke, haze operations only, generators or pots (2)	Yes
Smoke grenades	Yes
Incendiary devices to include trip flares	No
Star clusters/parachute flares	Yes
HC smoke of any type	No
Digging:	
Tank ditches	No
Hasty individual fighting positions, hand digging only, filled after use	Yes
Deliberate individual fighting positions	No